"We're often tempted to [...] we see all around us—po[...] Adamson rightly reminds [...] [...]uggle is often with hopelessness. In *Hope Breaks Through*, he gives a powerful invitation to overcome this spiritual poverty and help others do the same, without sugarcoating the world we live in."

Mark Batterson, *New York Times* bestselling author, *The Circle Maker*; lead pastor, National Community Church

"Before I read a book, I ask two basic questions: Does the author have credibility? And do they have something meaningful to say? Author Heath Adamson scores on both counts. His book *Hope Breaks Through* offers a fresh approach to a timely topic. This book will help you better understand the ways and purposes of God. On a scale of 1 to 10, this is a 10."

Hal Donaldson, founder and CEO, Convoy of Hope

"*Hope Breaks Through* compels us to step into our calling as the hands and feet of Jesus in a broken world. With compassion and clarity, Heath Adamson shares the profound truth that the hope we carry is not meant to be kept to ourselves but shared as a living testament of God's mercy and love. This book is a powerful reminder that when God's Spirit works in and through us, we become agents of change— bringing light to darkness, healing to the hurting, and hope to the hopeless. This is not just a book; it's a call to action!"

Daniela Freidzon McCabe, pastor, King of Kings, Buenos Aires, Argentina

"In a world that often feels paralyzed by hopelessness, Heath Adamson's words serve as both a beacon of light and a call to action. With deep biblical insight and inspiring stories, this book reminds us that hope is not a distant dream but a present, transformative force. Adamson challenges us to step out of our comfort zones, to exchange what is for what could be, and to partner with God in making a tangible difference in our world. His message is clear: Hope is not passive—it is a catalyst for change. I wholeheartedly recommend this book to anyone longing to rediscover the power of hope in their lives and communities."

Rev. Samuel Rodriguez, author; lead pastor, New Season; president and CEO, National Hispanic Christian Leadership Conference

"In *Hope Breaks Through*, Heath challenges us to not so easily give up our rightful inheritance as children of God, which is the ability to hope in him once more. Through telling powerful and redemptive stories that reveal God's faithfulness to those who trust and believe, Heath walks us through an insightful scriptural journey of the power of hope so that we, as God's children, can be used and blessed by the Lord more than ever before!"

Al Toledo, lead pastor, Chicago Tabernacle

"*Hope Breaks Through* is a transformative read, where Adamson masterfully draws from his personal world travels as well as Bible stories to reveal hope as the spiritual inheritance of every believer. His reflections powerfully demonstrate a reminder that even in dark and desperate circumstances, hope remains an ever-shining light."

Rob Hoskins, president, OneHope

"Indifference and fear cease where love is in action; hope abides where there is knowledge and wisdom. We need to be a people who create an environment of hope that can help people move away from despondency and move toward optimism about their future. Heath encourages us to change focus and see a God who thinks differently about us."

Rev. Philip Kitoto, general superintendent, Kenya Assemblies of God; chair, Evangelical Alliance of Kenya

HOPE
BREAKS
THROUGH

HOPE

BREAKS

THROUGH

HOW TO SEE BEYOND YOUR LIFE AND PUT
COMPASSION INTO ACTION

HEATH ADAMSON

BakerBooks

a division of Baker Publishing Group
Grand Rapids, Michigan

Published by Baker Books
a division of Baker Publishing Group
Grand Rapids, Michigan
BakerBooks.com

Printed in the United States of America

Library of Congress Cataloging-in-Publication Data
Names: Adamson, Heath, 1977– author.
Title: Hope breaks through : how to see beyond your life and put compassion into action / Heath Adamson.
Description: Grand Rapids, Michigan : Baker Books, a division of Baker Publishing Group, [2025] | Includes bibliographical references.
Identifiers: LCCN 2024038997 | ISBN 9781540903723 (paperback) | ISBN 9781540904676 (casebound) | ISBN 9781493449040 (ebook)
Subjects: LCSH: Hope—Religious aspects—Christianity. | Compassion—Religious aspects—Christianity.
Classification: LCC BV4638 .A34 2025 | DDC 234/.25—dc23/eng/20250106
LC record available at https://lccn.loc.gov/2024038997

Some names and details have been changed to protect the privacy of the individuals involved.

The author is represented by The Christopher Ferebee Agency, www.christopherferebee.com.

To the God of hope,
who stands with his children in the ruins
and invites them to dream again.

CONTENTS

INTRODUCTION

I walked into a leper colony for the first time with no idea what to expect.

Outside of its walls, children ran up and down the dirt roads chasing one another. Motorbikes dodged in and out of the bumper-to-bumper traffic. Peddlers at roadside stands sold fruits, bicycle tires, and live chickens. We knocked on the gate a few times before getting the guard's attention. Two eyes briefly peered at my traveling companion and me through what appeared to be a bullet hole. Multiple shrieks of rusty hinges grinding against one another and a few loud phrases in an unknown language preceded the slow roll of the green door. It was opened just enough to walk in and then quickly bolted shut again.

Across the open yard, a few dozen men stared at us as we walked toward them. Some of them slowly moved in our direction. One man approached us quickly. While his smile was radiant, the rest of his body revealed his broken physical condition. He was a leper.

The horrendous disease ate the tips of his fingers away. Sores covered his body with a blend of gray, purple, and red wounds. His eyes were vacant. The disease not only harmed him but isolated him as well. A few feet away, I smelled the rotting flesh. I started to dry heave.

I was embarrassed at my natural reflex. I leaned to my left and hunched over, trying to gain some sort of composure while convulsing. I had every intention of greeting him with the dignity he deserved, and I blew it. I was so ashamed. This man's outer appearance was a mere glimpse compared to what he must have experienced socially, emotionally, and spiritually. In that split second, my heart and mind wandered to the story of Jesus having a similar experience with a leper in Matthew 8. He responded much differently than I did. In that story, Jesus healed the leper.

I can only imagine what it would be like for someone living in utter hopelessness to come into contact with Jesus. No longer suffering social stigmatization and intense loneliness, the healed man would have fresh anticipation for a new day. The leper Jesus healed would likely return home and embrace his family again. He would need to learn to walk into crowded rooms in a different way. He would return to the basic things in life that, for a leper, had become luxuries.

It's important to note that before Jesus healed the leper, he did something equally as remarkable. He touched the leper.

Touching the leper reveals so many things about what God is like. God heals us in a way we understand. God notices and goes above and beyond to restore dignity and value to those he loves. His initial reflex is to reach out to us even if we are unable, ashamed, or just too discouraged to truly reach out to him. And the best part is there is no situation and no person who will ever be beyond God's grasp.

I stopped dry heaving and gained my composure. Looking up, he was standing right there. Gratefully, my reaction didn't drive him away. He was still smiling, waiting, not for me to hug him but, likely, for him to hug me. This is what hope looks like—confident and full of joy in the waiting. Remembering how Jesus touched the leper, all foregone conclusions of leprosy being extremely dangerous and contagious left my mind. In that moment, I did only what I knew to do. What you would do. What Jesus did.

I took a step toward him and extended my arms. Wrapping our arms around one another, I made sure to hold on tight enough and long enough to let love do its work. Not just in him. In me as well. There are a multitude of moments in my life when I should have responded in love more quickly. This is one I didn't miss. I never want to miss another one.

One of the best hugs I've ever received came from that man whose name I do not know. But I will never forget him. While we held one another, I prayed for his healing. When I let go, he was still leprous. But a different type of healing took place—in him and in me. I saw it in his eyes. I felt it in my heart.

Most of us can't relate to how a leper feels; however, we have more in common with them than we will ever realize. In 2 Kings 5, we are introduced to a man called Naaman. He is described as a mighty warrior and a man of valor. Underneath his armor, though, was a secret. Naaman was a leper. Like him, on the outside we may also appear successful and thriving as if the cares of this life or the very real worries in our world do not affect us. But underneath that veneer and despite the perceptions of others, we too may desperately struggle.

Hopelessness is not a condition people reach only when they are at the end of their rope. It is incremental, comes in many subtle shapes and sizes, and seeks to talk us out of pursuing our unshakable spiritual inheritance. It is deeper than discouragement. Hopelessness has a large appetite, and it grows increasingly hungry. We all face situations that seem too big, too impossible, and too painful to endure. We struggle to reconcile them with the God we thought we knew. Somewhere along the way, we begin to hope less and less, and eventually we wonder if God is still willing and able to touch what seems untouchable in our lives.

Our world and the church are full of people who are deeply discouraged. Hoping in God again—or for the first time—just feels too risky or impossible. What do you do after you cried out to God, wept, prayed, and longed for something to change, and it didn't? Or after you placed your hope in God only to walk away confused, disappointed, and even defeated? Or after you put yourself out there, trying to be part of the solution to the many problems that are destroying our generation, only to feel like your efforts weren't enough?

Most of us would never blatantly accuse God of letting us down or of not responding to our cry. But we subtly accuse him by being less vulnerable with him. We pray less, ignoring the dimly burning wick in our soul. We dream with him less often. We tolerate something inferior to what he promised us. We ignore our very real and present pain and camouflage it with religious jargon. Our world is falling apart, and we simply say, "God is still good."

But God is looking for something different. He wants our very real, unfiltered admittance that things seem too hard and too impossible or that no one can do anything about how bad things have gotten. But like the leper, we can stand confidently in the waiting. Hope gets to work and vulnerably, audaciously invites us to trust God again, acknowledging the way things are without allowing them to eclipse who God is.

14

A hope like this is not passive but active. It is not weak; it is mountain moving. It breaks through.

That's what this book is about: daring to see the God of hope reach out to you in your untouchable situation, inviting you to let go of what is and take hold of what could be. In Genesis 21, we read of the outcast servant Hagar when she and her helpless child were alone, homeless, and desperate. She longed for water in a dry and barren land. God visited her and opened her eyes, and she saw a water well. She wasn't blind; her eyes functioned perfectly. The answer to her heart's cry was right in front of her, yet in her hopelessness, she simply didn't see. God drew near to her, and she responded. God sees what we don't. When we dare to hope in God, we see things as they truly are.

All over the world in some of the most desperate places, I've seen the power of hope utterly shatter impossibilities. And I have also experienced how hope has broken through in my own life. It can happen in yours too.

We all see situations in our lives, families, communities, and across our world that are concerning and heartbreaking, make us fearful, and do not line up with God's character and promises. God invites us not to ignore the way things are but to refuse to allow them to define what could be. This is why hope is powerful.

Throughout our time together in this book, you will come face-to-face with the God of hope who walks through refugee camps across sub-Saharan Africa, among malnourished children in remote villages, and who draws near to you even now. The stories of ordinary heroes and the divine interruptions in the midst of extreme circumstances will reveal what hope can do in us, and even more importantly, through us.

In the first half of the book, we will take an honest look at what we all share in common across the human experience: We are all spiritually poor without hope in God. This form of poverty convinces us to do the unthinkable, seduces us to become self-dependent, and inhibits our view as we magnify our personal struggles over God's great invitation. No one regrets courageously, vulnerably placing their hope in God. Hope is not something we need simply to get through the hard times. It is a predisposition of the heart that acknowledges that surrendering to God is not a sign of weakness; it is the strongest thing we can ever do.

You will catch a glimpse of God's heart for you, and this, my friend, will apprehend you in a remarkable way. He wants you to see him for who he really is as hope gets to work, changing you long before your situation does. Hope must produce its fruit where you currently are in life before the next chapter of God's story can unfold. As you read, you'll discover that your time with God must be real, honest, and at times hard.

The second half of the book is about cultivating a lifestyle of hope as our inheritance in God becomes real. This will make the nearness of God your new reality. You will find meaning, see clearly, and develop the strength to endure. Impossibilities will no longer intimidate you. God will divinely interrupt you, draw near to where you are, and open your eyes to what is possible. Your relationship with God will grow increasingly intimate as you find joy in surrender and peace in trust. With a spiritual inheritance that is more than enough, you will find greater significance in taking your place at this juncture on the timeline of history. Life is too short to be consumed with the broken places in your past and the uncertainties of your present. Our world is crying out for hope to run wild in the streets. You can partner with

God to affect the type of change that will matter in the end. Like the leper Jesus healed, we can all become living stories of who God is and what he can do. The time is now, and the right choice is obvious. It may not be easy, but in the end, it will be worth it.

SECTION 1

SPIRITUAL POVERTY

1

A DESPERATE NEED FOR HOPE

"I sold my oldest daughter," he said.

As soon as those words filled the air, I was speechless. There is no word for what I felt. Had I heard him correctly? No father should ever reach a place like that, so utterly hopeless that he resorts to selling his child. It is something so unthinkable, so unspeakable, that I cringe even now as I remember his words.

"I sold my oldest daughter to buy food for the rest of my family."

The father felt he had little choice in a part of the world where malnutrition, hunger, and severe poverty strangle hope. I stood there unspeaking as a collision of sounds surrounded us. Loud buses barreled by. Motorbikes beeped. Men stood curbside and stared at nothing. Children too young to be unsupervised shouted at one another. We breathed in clouds of black smoke from trucks. I saw an elephant over my shoulder. A small brown monkey perched on the stone wall to my left. A body lay on the side of the road in a gutter. A multitude of children begged for food and money on the streets, most with physical deformities. Later, I found out they were not all born this way. Rather, as newborns, their brittle bones were manipulated by soulless individuals to make a long life of begging more profitable. Slavery is still rampant in our world.

I was in the middle of hell on earth. Hundreds of thousands call it home.

I remember losing focus, unable or perhaps unwilling to come to terms with what I just heard. As a husband and a father of two daughters, I simply cannot imagine selling one of my children. I was angry but not with the father. I was overwhelmed. I can still see his face. White and black whiskers jutted out from his weathered skin. His yellow eyes pierced a world others could not see. His fingernails, black from his toil in the landfill, were a stark contrast to the shiny black luxury car I saw in the distance. His clothes, torn, stained, and soiled, made him seem otherworldly. But he wasn't. He is someone whom God loves deeply. This father is someone like you and me.

At the time, I couldn't think of a response that didn't seem trite or maybe rehearsed. He didn't need me to ask him to bow his head, close his eyes, and repeat a prayer. He needed hope. I'm embarrassed to admit I didn't fully know what that would look like.

In that moment, I had plenty of food in my refrigerator. He scavenged to find scraps for his children. My suitcase had a clean pair of clothes to wear. His appearance and odor made it abundantly clear he had very little of anything. It appeared we had nothing in common. Yet I soon realized we did share something: There was only one place both of us could go to find hope.

As we stood facing one another on that street, what we both needed was for God to come and stand right there between us and pull heaven to earth.

The father carried his choice in his soul every morning, afternoon, and evening. His words to me were not an explanation or excuse. They were a confession, a reaching out to see what God could or would do. As the father and I talked about God and hope, he had a choice to make: Would he let the pain and heartbreak of his reality harden his heart even further? Or, in his vulnerability, would he look beyond where he was and let hope in?

I told him that, in essence, most choices are irreversible and many consequences unbearable, but there is a way forward even when life seems impossible. I watched his face change as he courageously chose to place his hope in God. After we prayed, his eyes seemed a little lighter and his smile unrestrained. His problems didn't go away. Placing our hope in God doesn't change everything. It can silence the voice of hopelessness though.

In my work around the world with Convoy of Hope, I have gazed into the eyes of war-shocked refugees, held malnourished children in my arms, and listened to young girls trapped under the unbearable burden of inequality. I've spoken with those who survived trafficking as they journeyed through trauma and began to find peace. And I've heard the cries of hungry infants born into famine. Whether you are in a remote village, alongside a river flowing with open sewage in the world's largest slums, or in your own neighborhood, hopelessness has the same gaze regardless of whose eyes it looks through. It stared at me through the eyes of college students, the wealthy, the famous, and the lonely. I've seen it in the mirror before too.

Hopelessness is not bound by age, class, or status. Neither is hope. I'm wholeheartedly convinced of the power of hope because I've seen the evidence time and time again. You can experience hope in your life too, and it can flow through you to others.

An Impostor

Like the father who sold his daughter, perhaps you are in a place where you have lost hope. You may not relate to his extreme situation, but hopelessness has no bias. If you compare your heartbreak, concern, or pain to someone else's, you may feel as though you have no right to feel the way you do. But God doesn't evaluate his level of concern for you by comparing you with others. God understands exactly where you are and how you got there.

Hopelessness knocks on the door of the human heart while folding laundry, when watching an athletic event, after a business deal, or while trying to fall asleep. Maybe you are recovering from abuse, barely making it financially, looking for help, sitting in isolation, struggling in a difficult marriage, healing from trauma, or hiding an addiction. You need hope but aren't quite sure where God is or how to turn toward him. Maybe you once looked toward God only to feel disappointed or betrayed. Now, though hope is needed to move forward, it's hard to find the courage to hope again. For others, you're already aware God sees you and cares, yet the struggle to reconcile the Jesus you fell in love with and your current circumstance is very real. And for still others, God often seems far away if not entirely indifferent.

You may not relate to someone whose overwhelming sense of helplessness is intimidating, but deep down, you know humanity was designed for more than its current struggle. Hopelessness runs rampant in homes, during pivotal moments of decision, and across all political aisles, and it hijacks almost every news story. Fears related to disease, terrorism, war, prejudice, job loss, the health and well-being of those we love, and climate shock prevail.

I'm not OK with this. I suspect you aren't either.

We want to take personal responsibility for the lack of hope in the world because we care, are motivated to confront injustice with the kindness of God, and are compelled by our love for God to love our neighbor too. Often we feel like I did as I stood before that hopeless father—we don't know where to begin.

When we become indifferent, apathetic, or paralyzed by fear of failure, this too is a form of hopelessness. The size of the need intimidates us. In the end, we are all familiar with the overwhelming sense of hopelessness around us. Hopelessness transcends borders and creeps into living rooms, office buildings, classrooms, and social media. Why?

Hopelessness comes from failing to see the God of hope who is already working on our behalf. But hopelessness is an impostor. It doesn't belong. With God, we can all do something to silence its claims.

Hope is much more powerful than the impostor of hopelessness. Hope is a fundamental human need. It is also a human right. When you take away an athlete's mobility, you injure them. When you take away someone's income, you inhibit them. When you rob someone's hope, you destroy them. It seems as if our spiritual adversary is less concerned with our faith and more focused on our hope. He will do everything he can to render us hopeless.

The voice of hope speaks up and interrupts our hopeless spiral. If we vulnerably respond to its beckoning, it will bring to us God's promise of peace. Your dream may be to start a new family legacy and end the cycle of divorce. Or for the vicious cycle of addiction to end once and for all. Some of us long to experience healing from trauma and abuse. Others want to use their experience to see real transformation occur in the lives of others. They just need a little help getting there.

We all have dreams planted in the soil of our hearts. God put them there. Tragically, the epidemic of hopelessness has convinced many that the dreams are gone or that they aren't worth pursuing. In the end, multitudes simply feel alone in their deepest struggle.

Never Alone

Chastity Patterson received a response from her dad four years after her father passed away.

At the age of twenty-three, she could no longer share a cup of coffee, go on a stroll in the park, or watch a game with her dad. He hadn't been her biological father, but he was more of a dad to her than anyone else. After all, he was the one to confront her attitude when it was bad. He attended her games, was present for school dances, even prom. When her boyfriend came over, her dad protected her.

Losing someone you love who is a trustworthy voice on your journey leaves a void. After her father's passing, Chastity continued to text his cell phone every day with thoughts, concerns, regrets, and random updates. She reflected on her efforts at self-care and her victorious fight against cancer. She updated him on her feelings for a young man. When her heart was broken, she told her dad all about it. After graduating with honors from college, she made sure to let her dad know. The texting went on for nearly four years. Of course, she knew her dad wasn't on the other end of the text thread. It just helped to talk to him as if he were listening.

That is when she received a text message from her deceased father's phone.

The night before the four-year anniversary of his passing, Chastity sent a text outlining how her Friday was going to be a challenge. A few days later, a response came from her deceased father's cell phone. "My name is Brad and I lost my daughter in a car wreck August 2014 and your messages have kept me alive. When you text me, I know it's a message from God." Brad went on to say how he read the texts and listened to her heart, watching her grow through life's ups and downs. He said that he had wanted to text her back many times over the years, but fear of breaking Chastity's heart prevented him from doing so. Brad told her, "I'm sorry you have to go through this but if it makes it any better, I am very proud of you!" Someone was listening to the thoughts of her heart for years. She wasn't as alone as she thought.[1]

None of us are.

Hope in God embraces the reality that God is near even when he seems far away. It is simple, not simplistic. Maintaining hope isn't always easy. But hope is designed to be a traveling companion along difficult paths. Solomon wrote in the tenth century BC that "hope deferred makes the heart sick, but a desire fulfilled is a tree of life" (Prov. 13:12). The word *desire* is also translated as *longing*.

We are an evidence-based society. If evidence is seen, then it must be true, right? This is helpful when making a decision related to our health, our finances, or whether to buy new tires for the car. It is a lousy way to find hope because the human soul was designed to long for a God we don't see. Hebrews 11:1 tells us that faith is "the substance of things hoped for, the evidence of things not seen" (KJV). Longing and hope are designed to invite us to draw closer to God before there is evidence that our hope is not in vain.

Hope transforms our perspective and invites us to embrace God's promises with childlike wonder. Hope is looking for a person to agree with its audacious claims. It often requires the courage to be vulnerable before God and the honesty to be authentic. Hope always does its best work when accompanied by humility, faith, endurance, surrender, trust, and intimacy with God. We all have hope deep down inside. The hard part is allowing ourselves enough hope to dream again.

When the substance of our soul is exposed during difficult times, the familiar enemies of hope are there to greet us. Their names are shame and doubt, hopelessness and lack. They remind us of our insufficiencies, failures, and insecurities. They sound convincing, but they are falsehoods. Hope is always anchored in truth because hope comes from God.

So, what is hope, does it really make a difference, and how do you get it?

More Than a Wish

Hope impacts our emotions positively. In the workplace, self-efficacy, optimism, resilience, and hope positively impact productivity. "Hope accounts for 14 percent of productivity . . . more than intelligence, optimism, or self-efficacy."[2] It is predictive for athletes beyond training, confidence, and mood.[3] But hope isn't based on facts observed with the natural eye. As we will see, it is based on something greater.

Dr. Brené Brown says, "We need hope like we need air" and that hope isn't "a warm, fuzzy emotion that fills us with a sense of possibility. Hope is a way of thinking—a cognitive process."[4] She goes on to say hopelessness is an emotion, and it "arises out of a combination of negative life events, and negative thought patterns, particularly self-blame and the perceived inability to change our circumstances."[5] Hope, she says, isn't an emotion but a function.

Sociologist Peter Berger describes hope as a sign of something transcendent or otherworldly because of the "secularization of consciousness."[6] It is the recognition that something or someone outside of the here and now is interrupting us. We aren't alone when we hope. Plato viewed hope as something rational. To him, it was not for people who can't deal with reality and, for this reason, drift off into a fantasyland. It is not denial of one's circumstance even when it is painful or disappointing.[7] Arthur Brooks said hope is "believing you can make things better without distorting reality."[8] Emily Dickinson artistically described it this way:

> "Hope" is the thing with feathers
> That perches in the soul,
> And sings the tune without the words
> And never stops at all.[9]

Many people associate hope with having a strong inner core, being emotionally resilient, and demonstrating agency. Søren Kierkegaard described hope as being essential. Kant said one of the three questions that reside within reason is "what may I hope?" *The Stanford Encyclopedia of Philosophy* says, "Hope is not only an attitude that has cognitive components—it is responsive to facts about the possibility and likelihood of future events. It also has a conative component—hopes are different from mere expectations insofar as they reflect and draw upon our desires."[10] Aristotle taught that hope requires courage.[11] It's true. We must be courageous enough to pay attention to our desires and dreams when they seem unattainable or far away.

While some of these definitions are insightful and certainly frame our understanding, there is more to hope. God is the author of it, and we all need it. Why? Because discouragement and overwhelm are legitimate things to feel when our situation warrants it. They are lousy places to stay though.

29

In John 16:33 Jesus said, "In the world you will have tribulation. But take heart; I have overcome the world."

First, notice God tells us up front that life will be hard. We shouldn't be waiting for the sky to fall. But when it does, we don't blame God. Simply put, sometimes disappointment, overwhelm, and heartbreak do occur.

Secondly, God makes it clear that tribulation and difficulty aren't the end of the story because he has already overcome the world. That's good news. It means there is another chapter to the story, and that chapter is much, much better than the one you, the father in the slum, and everyone else is currently in.

Sandwiched between both of these truths—life being hard and Jesus overcoming—is a simple instruction. Jesus didn't say to ignore reality. He says, "But take heart." As humans, we are designed to connect our circumstances to our feelings. When life is hard, faith doesn't ignore it. Faith says there is another chapter to the story. In order to get there, hope speaks up and asks us to "take heart." Hope is not circumstantial. It doesn't ignore the very real pain we experience, but it does change how we experience it. It is the beginning of the greater reality to live in.

Dr. Henry Cloud put it this way: "The difference between hoping and wishing is that hope comes from real, objective reasons that the future is going to be different from the past. Anything other than that is simply a wish that comes from your desires."[12] Hope, according to 1 Peter 1:3–4 is the presence of our future inheritance—here and now. Hope is less about our understanding of what the future holds and more about the certainty of God's involvement in it. This profoundly shapes how we respond when life feels hopeless.

Choose Now

What we see is not all there is. When we have hope in God, the eyes of our hearts are opened to a new way of understanding. This is how Abraham, against all hope, was still able to believe (Rom. 4:18). He used the tiniest seed of hope as a starting point to believe God for something greater to come.

When we rely on our own reasoning and insist on seeing before we wholeheartedly believe, we will likely miss most of what God is up to. Someone once put it this way: "Seeing is not necessarily believing. With God, believing is seeing." We know we are not alone and that we are all under the watchful eye of a loving God. Our prayers are cherished, not balked at. Our dreams are seen by him, not ignored. God is why we can choose to reject the inevitability of pain and injustice as our final destination. Yes, we will have trouble in life (John 16:33). But life and trouble are temporary. You can choose today to partner with what will endure forever for the benefit of your own life, those you love, and your generation. We are born again to a living hope.

In the Psalms, we see an example of how we acknowledge our current experiences in light of the hope we have: "Why are you cast down, O my soul . . . ? Hope in God" (42:11). The psalmist is vulnerable with his emotions and authentic with his feelings. He does not deny his reality. Yet he is courageous in hope. He acknowledges where he is at. He even speaks to himself, his very own soul, and attempts to bend his heart in the right direction. He summons himself to that place. What is the object of his affection? Where is he asking his hope to fix its eyes? God. He tells his soul to put his hope in God.

I was in town for work, near a friend's home, and we went out for breakfast to catch up. While we were eating, I asked him how he would describe or define *hope*. He told me the story of how he introduced the concept to his young children. He began by telling them that they were going to get ice cream soon. Immediately, the kids beamed. Mentioning ice cream again later in the day only brought more exuberance and anticipation. They giggled, smiled, and were full of joy. By the time they ate ice cream, not only did the kids enjoy the moment but their dad did too. My friend told me that hope is "experiencing the joy of something before you actually experience it."

A child can hear a promise and vulnerably allow joy to come without the fear of "what if." Ice cream in the future is just as real to a child as if a giant bowl of it were already in front of them. This shows me they have a father who is trustworthy. They experienced the joy of ice cream before they tasted it.

Dr. Caroline Leaf, in her book *Switch On Your Brain*, says, "Thoughts are real, physical things that occupy mental real estate."[13] It is in this space where our hope is influenced. She goes on to say, "What you think and how you understand yourself—your beliefs, dreams, hopes, and thoughts—has a huge impact on how your brain works."[14] But she is not advocating we hope in ourselves. She doesn't suggest we put our hope in *hope*. She says, "You can be happy and filled with peace regardless of your circumstances."[15] Like the psalmist said, put your hope in God.

How does God define hope?

A Promise Made Is a Promise Kept

According to Strong's concordance, the Hebrew word *tikvah* or *tiqwah* is translated into English as "hope."[16] *Tikvah* is found in some of the Scriptures we carry with us in our hearts, like Jeremiah 29:11 where God's plan is to "give you a future and a hope [*tikvah*]." Jeremiah 31:17 says, "There is hope [*tikvah*] for your future, declares the LORD." Hope is closely linked to our future but begins and ends with God. Romans 15:13 says, "May the God of hope fill you with all joy and peace as you trust in him, so that you may overflow with hope by the power of the Holy Spirit" (NIV). The God of hope fills us with joy and peace for a reason: so that we may "overflow with hope." He gives us joy because we don't have to wait until everything changes to move forward, and he gives us peace because he knows how hard it can be.

Overflowing with hope does not come naturally for any of us. This is why we must live supernaturally by the power of the Holy Spirit. When we do this, there is a divine exchange, and God's will is done on earth as it already is in heaven. God uses *hope* as an adjective to describe himself. He positions himself as the Creator and reward of it. If God has hope, we should too. When we hope, God draws near. He provides supernatural power to achieve his purpose, which is that we may overflow with hope.

If the impact of hope in God was completely up to God, our future would be a beautiful guarantee. However, God is not the only one involved in the conversation. We all have a responsibility to hold on to our end of the rope. Proverbs 23:18 says, "Surely there is a future, and your hope will not be cut off." It's very important to understand the phrase "cut off." It describes both our responsibility and God's when it comes to what hope can do. And it comes from a story you wouldn't necessarily think of to describe what hope really looks like. The story is found in Joshua 2 as Israelite soldiers are on a reconnaissance mission before the battle of Jericho.

While in the city conducting ancient spycraft, the cover for the Israeli spies was blown. The king of Jericho hunted them. If found, they would be imprisoned or killed. The spies found refuge in the home of Rahab, a prostitute and a sworn enemy of any Israelite. Rather than turn them in, Rahab did something remarkable. She helped them escape. In exchange, she and her household would receive a great reward. They said to her:

> "Behold, when we come into the land, you shall tie this scarlet cord in the window through which you let us down, and you shall gather into your house your father and mother, your brothers, and all your father's household." . . . And she said, "According to your words, so be it." Then she sent them away, and they departed. And she tied the scarlet cord in the window. (Josh 2:17–18, 21)

In other words: Because you helped us, you and your family will survive when we come back with our army. And in order to survive the impending invasion we have one instruction for you to keep. Tie this cord in the window. This cord will be a symbol to the soldiers not to harm you or your family. We keep our promises. Even amid indescribable chaos and war, we will keep our word to you.

You'll notice in these three verses in Joshua 2 that the word *hope* doesn't appear in our English translations. That's because *tikvah*, the same word for hope, is translated as "cord."[17] The metaphor behind hope is that of a cord or rope. The rope tying us to God's promises is far from weak and tattered. It is tightly woven together and meticulously crafted. That's why it is so dependable and strong. So strong, soldiers can scale a building with it. The cord symbolizes how a promise made, after a time of waiting, is a promise kept. Rahab eventually married Salmon, an Israelite, and had a son named Boaz (the husband of Ruth). Joseph, the earthly father of Jesus, is her descendant. Rahab is in the genealogy of Jesus of Nazareth (Matt. 1:5).

Rahab's hope ties together the conquest of Jericho, the amazing story of generosity and love recorded in the book of Ruth, and even the family Jesus himself grew up in. A bright future means your cord remains uncut. Literally, regardless of how difficult things are, we need to hold on to the hope we have and make sure it is never cut off. We hold on, not for fear of falling but because by doing so we can climb higher and higher. Like Rahab, even when everything around us is about to crumble as the walls of Jericho did, we can focus on the promise. What we choose to see during the hard times matters.

Turn Aside

In Exodus 3, an eighty-year-old shepherd named Moses is tending sheep in a place called Horeb. After forty long years of wandering in the desert, he experienced a divine interruption. Earlier in his life, Moses had murdered an Egyptian man. As a fugitive on the run for decades, he certainly didn't seem qualified to receive an invitation from God to do anything. (Then again, none of us are.) Despite delayed promises in his life and decades of baggage to sift through, Moses lifted his eyes from his circumstances and looked toward something better, something deeper.

In the story, God lights a bush on fire and waits for Moses— like he often waits for us. He is patient. Moses sees the bush, slows down, and decides to "turn aside to see this great sight" (v. 3). What seems like just another mundane moment is now different. He *sees* the bush in a different way. The word we translate as "see" is *raah*.[18] It means to see and also to perceive and understand.[19] It is sort of like seeing not only with

35

physical eyes but also with the eyes of the heart. All moments can be like this. Why? God is here and there right now.

Also notice that God speaks to Moses only after Moses turns aside. Sometimes God withholds his voice until we slow down long enough to see what is right in front of us. As Moses struggles with insecurity and discouragement, he asks for God's name (vv. 13–14). In our English Bibles, we translate God's name as "I am who I am." We use a present tense to translate what, in Hebrew, is technically a future tense. It literally means "I will be what I will be." God identifies with Moses in a place that was beyond his current experience. It is almost as if God says, "Moses, I obviously know your past, and I found you today, but there is something remarkable and beautiful you are unaware of. It isn't here; it's there. Here, take my hand. Let's do this together." God is never finished in our situation either if the promise is still future tense. We can place our hope in God because God isn't just here—he is already there. That's where our hope is tethered. Moses eventually leaves Horeb and travels to Egypt where he partners with God to bring hope to others.

Ancient religions believed the uncertainty of tomorrow could be discovered in the stars far away. The God of hope came and walked among us. Over the years, others reduced the creation of life to mere chance, yet God is never surprised. While some look toward political views to find their security, we have a Father in heaven. Multitudes hoard money for a sense of stability, but God already knows what we will need. Relational networks are often a source of assurance for the hopeless, but remember, God knows your name. Education can be valuable, but knowledge and information change. God never does.

Science places the future of our world at the feet of genetic mutation, but God forms galaxies with his voice. Hope cannot ultimately be found in this world. It is tied to God alone.

Like Moses, you can have hope regardless of what you're facing. Burning bushes are found by fathers in the world's slums, through text messages, and even in the pages of a book. This book ultimately isn't about what I have to say. The message is about you and the God who sees you, knows you, and invites you to turn aside as well. I am not a perfect person with all the answers. I do, however, have some experience watching hope break through insurmountable situations. What I've personally seen God do in some of the most desperate places on earth—and in my own life—is unforgettable. If God can do it then and there, God can do it anywhere.

2

SPIRITUAL POVERTY

Impossible is a word used by those who forget God still walks among us. Sometimes I still forget.

In one of the most isolated and impoverished places on earth, God reintroduced me to what hope truly is and what poverty really looks like.

The village in Indonesia was extremely difficult to reach. A torrential river separated it from the rest of civilization. Extreme poverty was normal. With no clean water, no electricity, no outside income, and barely enough food, almost everyone was malnourished. To put this into perspective, village elders, grown men in their sixties, were the size of ten-year-old boys because of stunting. Then Convoy of Hope, where I serve vocationally, got involved. We worked with the elders and installed a water well. The remote location prevented the use of modern equipment, so after thirty days of digging by hand, clean water finally arrived. The village leader smiled as he scooped up pure water in his hands for a drink.

Now there is plenty of food for everyone, sustainable income for families, clean water, solar-powered electricity, and a school where the children are thriving. The village experienced a spiritual renewal and then built a church. Underneath all the transformation, something else was going on, something deeper.

On my way to check on the village with part of the team from Convoy of Hope, I severely sprained both of my ankles. The soles of my feet were black and purple, and my ankles were the size of grapefruit. I was in pain and could barely walk. Yet I was determined to get there as I didn't travel halfway around the world simply to turn back. When we arrived at the river's edge, ready to swim or walk on tiptoes, the village gathered on the other side. They came for three reasons: to thank us for coming, to show us the way through the hills to their village, and to help me cross.

The village leader came up behind me, put his hand on my arm, and pointed ahead. I will never forget what happened next. I saw what hope looks like, and it arrived just in time.

A young man came down the hill holding an old wooden chair. Some elders, holding poles, accompanied him. They crossed the river, strapped me into the chair, affixed the poles to it, and carried me to the other side. The current was swift. The distance long. They worked hard. They cheered and sang songs the entire way. Even though I cringed from the pain in my ankles, I felt like Indiana Jones! I laughed and cried, humbled by a simple act of kindness from some of the poorest people in the world.

Beyond the river, the terrain was too unstable to carry me, so a village elder gave me a walking stick and other men walked beside me. We arrived in the village and held a ceremony. We drank water from coconuts. The one translator struggled to keep up with the conversation. Some things, like hugs and laughter, needed no translation. We stood in the middle of nowhere, together, and gave thanks to God for the water well, the community transformation, and the hope everyone in the village had. Then the elders told us about other villages nearby. They wanted them to experience hope too.

The Hand on Your Shoulder

Poverty is one of many results of hopelessness reproducing itself through individuals, governments, religions, economies, and patterns. The poverty I describe throughout this book and devote my life to eradicating is an observable reality of a broken world. Broken lives. Broken trust. Broken promises.

Poverty isn't just found in the poorest places on earth, however. It is also found within us all. We each have a form of poverty that is much deeper than economic statistics or educational opportunities. It is spiritual. In no way am I denigrating people or making real-life vulnerabilities seem light. Instead, I am standing on the bank of the river with you, admitting that without God there is no way we will ever get where we need to go.

George Orwell put it this way:

> A rather cruel trick I once played on a wasp. He was sucking jam on my plate and I cut him in half. He paid no attention, merely went on with his meal, while a tiny stream of jam trickled out of his severed esophagus. Only when he tried to fly away did he grasp the dreadful thing that had happened to him. It is the same with us. The thing that has been cut away is our soul and there is a period of time . . . during which we do not notice it.[1]

A wealthy and thriving businesswoman may not scavenge for food, but she too can struggle with hopelessness. The single parent, working two jobs while raising kids, feels invisible and is painstakingly lonely. The student, bullied on social media and sitting alone at school or even in church, needs more than an increase in spending money. The praying grandparent, longing for the fentanyl addiction to stop pushing their grandchild down a path of self-destruction, would give anything just to see freedom come. Christians all over struggle deeply to reconcile the current state of their relationship with God with what they hope is accessible one day.

Most forms of poverty are not financial. Some of the poorest people in the world seem like the wealthiest. What do I mean? I've sat around many fires in remote villages listening to the sound of singing and laughter. These people may not have clean water, electricity, or much food, but they still tell stories from their childhood and hold one another's children. The hospitality they show may not seem like much to an outside observer, but it is better than any five-star restaurant. In some ways, yes, they are poor. In other ways, they are rich.

They take you in as a stranger and make you part of their family. They prepare a table with milk from whatever animal they have and set a few pieces of fried dough, fruit, or root vegetables in front of you. On more than one occasion, people fed me the only chicken the village had. Refusing to eat such a delicacy is the greatest insult you could give. I sat there, watching the shadows from the flames crawl up the trees, as generations sang songs together and danced. Even though I was oblivious to what they were saying, I felt like I was among friends.

On the bank of that river, I had been completely discouraged. I didn't think I was going to make it across. But I wasn't alone. The hand on my shoulder diverted my attention upward. This is what hope does. It gently places a hand on our shoulders and helps us see beyond. God never leaves us to fend for ourselves. Once hope bears fruit in our lives, it transforms our perspective so that, like the elders, we are compelled to help others.

A safe assumption is that you do not find sustenance from a city dump nor live in extreme poverty. These forms of brokenness are completely wrong and unacceptable, and once exposed, they should move us to action. Indifference and apathy have no place in the life of someone who has been made spiritually alive because of the gospel. As you read this, it is my sincere prayer you will find a place to partner with God, through demonstrated love and compassion, to confront the illegitimacy of poverty. Do so, not just in the hard and remote places but wherever you find yourself today. Poverty was never part of God's original design, and we must never get used to it. James 1:27 is clear: "Religion that is pure and undefiled before God the Father is this: to visit orphans and widows in their affliction, and to keep oneself unstained from the world."

We have much to learn about what hope and true riches look like from others we deem poor. Henri Nouwen said, "This is our great challenge and consolation. Jesus comes to us in the poor, the sick, the dying, the prisoners, the lonely, the disabled, the rejected. There we meet him, and there the door to God's house is opened for us."[2]

Pure Gold and Dirty Water

Jesus describes spiritual poverty in Revelation 3:14–18. His words were directed to a literal church community existing two thousand years ago in the city of Laodicea. It was centrally located between two trade routes headed east/west and north/south. At the time, there was a somewhat wealthy, significant Jewish population in the city. Taxes to the temple in Jerusalem were paid in gold. In 62 BC, to stabilize the currency, the governor made exporting gold from the city illegal.

Much of the city's wealth came from a centralized banking system used by traders, a nearby medical training school specializing in eye salve, and exports of wool and carpet.[3] The inhabitants were wealthy enough that when an earthquake destroyed the city in AD 60, the locals refused funding from Rome as they had enough money of their own. In the *Annals*, Tacitus, a Roman historian, writes, "Laodicea arose from the ruins by the strength of her own resources and with no help from us."[4] The city had plenty of gold.

But they lacked water. Six miles north of the city were well-known hot springs in Hierapolis. Ten miles south, in Colossae, was a mountain stream that carried cold water. But in Laodicea, the local streams often dried up. The nearby Lycus river was too dirty to use. City engineers constructed underground aqueducts to source the locals with water. You can still see them to this day. Leftover residue in the stone pipes reveals that, by the time the water reached the city through the pipes, it was not very pure and tepid in temperature.

Using these two familiar circumstances—wealth and lack of life-sustaining water—Jesus describes the spiritual condition of the church in this city. He says to them, "I know your works: you are neither cold nor hot. Would that you were either cold or hot! So, because you are lukewarm, neither hot nor cold, I will spit you out of my mouth. For you say, I am rich, I have prospered, and I need nothing, not realizing that you are wretched, pitiable, poor, blind, and naked" (Rev. 3:15–17).

According to Jesus, the people of Laodicea aren't poor economically as they had plenty of gold and their economy was booming. The word Jesus uses for poor in Revelation means "destitute, spiritually poor."[5]

Jesus sees the people of Laodicea for who they truly are— spiritually poor and, like their aqueduct water, unappetizingly lukewarm. After Jesus speaks the truth to them, with every word grounded in love, he asks them to deal with their condition not through their own strengths and abilities but by coming to him.

I've seen thousands upon thousands of children who sit beside open sewage in slums all over the world. They are poor, some blind, and some even lack clothing. Imagine walking up to a child in that condition and asking them to go to Tiffany's and purchase some gold earrings or a necklace for you. The child wouldn't have the faintest idea what you were talking about, let alone have what was necessary to complete the transaction. A purchase like that would be simply impossible. You can't buy something of value when you don't have money. That's the point Jesus makes in verse 18. Their form of poverty cannot be resolved by anything this world has to offer.

A Knock at the Door

Spiritual poverty impacts our lives in various ways. First, it sabotages the power of hope. Like the Laodiceans, we say we don't need a thing. Denial like this is elusive because, in poverty of soul, lukewarmness often masquerades as contentment. We don't need to be vulnerable in hope because we think everything is just perfect. In essence, we have more faith in ourselves than God. We become the people who have access to resources and opportunities and whose lives appear to be successful—unfortunately, successful at what won't matter in the end. We have a deeper need that only God can meet. It is easy to assume that a father who sells his child is in a state of utter hopelessness and that he wouldn't do such a thing if he knew God was with him. The truth, though, is that anytime we take matters into our own hands to solve a situation that is hopeless, while Jesus is on the outside knocking, we are guilty of something just as unthinkable.

Priest and peace activist Philip Berrigan described our poverty of soul this way: "The poor remind us of who we are, and the prophets of who we should be. So, we hide the poor and kill the prophets."[6] A lack of self-awareness breeds hopelessness, and we don't know it. Jesus acknowledges the Laodiceans are spiritually poor and understands they can't purchase what he has to offer. They don't have the ability to get out of the situation they are in. No matter how hard we try, we can't escape spiritual poverty without God either.

The second impact spiritual poverty has on us is that it allows us to adopt a new and inferior normal. We get used to life without God. In our lack of self-awareness, we become self-dependent. We sit in an empty house pretending to have access to everything we need, oblivious to the fact that we've evicted God.

There was a time when God graciously invited us into relationship and we depended on him. He is the one who adopted us into his family and let us into a new spiritual home. We sat at his table and enjoyed his food. But then we became used to his blessing and forgot about him. We reached a point of self-sufficiency. We have Jesus—a spiritual inheritance worth trillions upon trillions upon trillions of dollars so to speak. Yet we leave Jesus's offer unclaimed and choose to drink our lukewarm water and make believe everything is fine.

How does Jesus confront this? He comes to us and gently, respectfully knocks on the door of our heart. He doesn't kick the door down and surround our houses with a SWAT team. He doesn't nail an eviction notice on the door. He stands at the door and knocks (Rev. 3:20).

I can imagine what happens after Jesus's knock. At first, the knock isn't heard because of the laughter and conversation within. Then someone who has an ear to hear catches a faint noise in the distance. It's someone knocking at the door.

"I wonder who it could be? Surely, it isn't Jesus. After all, we are in his house, enjoying his delicacies, seated at his table. He must be in here somewhere."

The knocking persists, not annoyingly but lovingly. He doesn't barge in but knocks, not to berate everyone for their callousness but because he still longs to be with us—even those who've grown lukewarm in their soul.

What if you were the one who finally got up, went to the door, and saw Jesus's eyes looking in through the peephole? Whether there was any lack of self-awareness in your heart before, in that moment, you would come face-to-face with your ever-present, never-ending need for God. The self-sufficiency that provided a false sense of hope would be revealed for what it truly is: inferior.

Jesus is knocking on the door of your heart now, wherever you are on your faith journey. Whether you feel spiritually filthy and overwhelmed with hopelessness or you think you have it all together and need nothing, open the door. He wants to come in.

Let's imagine you open the door and say, "Jesus, how did you get outside? I thought you were in here."

And he replies, "No, I left a while ago. I'm heartbroken you didn't notice I wasn't there. I said many times I would never leave you. Sometimes, though, you push me away. But

I couldn't forget you, so I came back. I've lost count of the times I stood here knocking with no answer. But today you heard me knock. You responded. You even opened the door. May I come in and share a meal with you?"

Recognizing our hopelessness without God is the beginning of real hope. Will we take what we know and what we think we know about God and life and go it alone? Or will we let God in? True significance begins when we realize that the resources we have on our own are not enough to provide what we truly need. But significance is fully realized when we live our lives with eternity in mind—making the most of each opportunity, one hope-filled moment at a time.

Hope was never intended to be a last resort when we reach the end of our rope. It is designed to shape the choices we make, the prayers we pray, and how we process our feelings.

Life will always be inferior without real hope (Eph. 1:18). Hopelessness is not found in remote villages alone. It is found wherever God's knock at the door remains unanswered. When challenges become familiar, no action or vulnerability on our part is required to deal with them. Hope, however, takes work. We must wrestle with our thoughts and feelings about our circumstances, humble ourselves, and exchange our desires for God's.

Do You See Me?

A few months ago, I visited a group of African villages of approximately 150,000 people. Half of the population was under the age of fifteen. The streets, filled with the stench of open sewage, were also full of stray dogs, mounds of trash, and some of the most beautiful children I had ever seen—70 percent of whom were HIV positive.

When I walked down the dusty roads, I noticed almost all of the men were gone. While some were off looking for work and others had abandoned their families, most died from complications related to AIDS. The children were sick because they didn't take the antiretroviral medicine the government provides. When taken properly, it not only lengthens life but profoundly improves the quality of it. The reason they didn't take the medicine was because it upset their stomachs. It's meant to be taken with food, and they didn't have enough food.

Approximately 1 percent of the children in the village will graduate high school. Why? It isn't that they are less intelligent or have fewer dreams. It is because they are sick, hungry, malnourished, do not have clean water, and live in poverty; most cannot even afford to buy a pencil.

There are places in the world where children don't smile, and their stares are lifeless. Where hope is a fossil in the human experience. Where hopelessness is thick and the burden is real. These are the places our team continues to serve. In places like these, God is at work, and the sound of hope is emerging.

When we arrived at the African village, the children gathered and began to sing of how good and marvelous God is. Convoy of Hope recently built a kitchen at the school and started a feeding program. The children were grateful to God because they had food. The administrator at the school pulled me aside and put it this way: "When you feed a child in this village, that child can be educated. It is like putting him or her on the roof of a building so he or she can say to the world, 'Here I am. Do you see me?'"

Wow. A plate of food provided opportunity for the children to receive an education, take medication, and begin to flourish. The children shouted that simple question to the world because they know they are of value, and they long to find their place in this world.

We are all like those children, longing to find our place and wondering if we are really seen by a loving God who audaciously stands at the door of each human heart and knocks. Even when you don't understand what is happening, he sees you. He knows your journey.

I See You

Our world struggles with what it means to be human. Artificial intelligence, biomedical engineering, nanotechnology, social pressures, and gene editing redefine aspects of who we think we are. We invest so much time trying to be seen, and when we are, we spend the rest of our time trying to remember who we were. We're taken by surprise when someone posts an undoctored photo online because authenticity and identity have become mere commodities. It has gotten to the point where we question what it truly means to be human.

Being human means we are created in God's image. Each one of us is seen, known, and loved by God. We can take all of our affection and desire and pour it out on him.

One of the main reasons we struggle to see with eyes of hope is not necessarily because we doubt God's ability. After all, God shaped the universe with his voice and parted the Red Sea. God can do anything. His ability isn't up for debate. Often what we question is his willingness to help. Financial pressures can ruin someone's ability to hope. Relational tension can staunch our progress. Fear can sabotage us as we wait around for tomorrow, which brings more disappointment. We believe God can help that other person but doubt his desire to help us. We simply feel alone. But like Chastity, who was being listened to all those years she sent text messages to her deceased father's phone, you aren't as alone as it may seem. We all have a heavenly Father who is listening to our concerns and is willing and able to help.

In Genesis 16, we meet Hagar, a woman who would certainly identify with our loneliness. She was an Egyptian slave to Abraham and Sarah. Even though Sarah was barren, God had promised them a child. After ten years of hoping in God, Sarah became desperate. In an attempt to cure her shame and lift the curse of her barrenness, she arranged for Hagar to become Abraham's concubine in order to produce a child. Hagar became pregnant and bore Abraham a son, and eventually Sarah was filled with jealousy.

When we attempt to fulfill the promises of God without God, we will never be at peace. Sarah severely mistreated Hagar. When the conflict in the home became too much, Abraham sent his firstborn child and Hagar into the desert. Hagar would have felt alone and broken in so many ways. Surrounded by emotional, relational, financial, and spiritual rubble, she experienced a collision between heaven and earth. Hope bloomed out of the dry and arid soil of despair.

At that point in history, from what we know, nobody on planet Earth knew how to describe or address God. No one yet knew his name. The one who spoke the universe into existence is not named in the creation account. He is simply called God. God, who created male and female in his image, named the humans (Gen. 5:1–2). The people, however, didn't give God a name. Noah invested over one hundred years of his life building a boat large enough to endure a global deluge. He did so simply out of response to a God who was, again, unnamed. God was known as, well, God (Gen. 6–8).

Something changes in Genesis 16 though. An abandoned slave named Hagar was left to survive on her own. She carried her child under a blistering sun in a treacherous climate.

She had no family to run to and no savings account to draw from. She was isolated and desperate. But God saw her and drew near. In quite possibly the most hopeless moment in her life, Hagar saw a God who was not only with her but who saw her as well.

Genesis 16:13 says, "So she called the name of the LORD who spoke to her, 'You are a God of seeing,' for she said, 'Truly here I have seen him who looks after me.'" We know something breathtaking about God, one of his names and attributes, because Hagar saw beyond her circumstance and found the God of hope.

Where Are You?

Through the story of Hagar, we know that God isn't just a thundering voice from heaven. We know he is a God who sees and who guarantees he will also come close, placing a hand on our shoulder, directing our attention toward what's coming. That is just who he is. Acknowledging that we are "wretched, pitiable, poor, blind, and naked" (Rev. 3:17) without God should motivate us to get up from the table, regardless of what feast is in front of us, and open the door to let God in.

Here, he looks you in the eyes, confirming over and over again that he sees not only everything you have been through but also sees you. You don't need to strive to be seen by God nor should you beg. Simply responding to the knock on the door of your heart is where hope begins to break through.

Some of us, however, don't struggle as much with God's willingness or ability to help. Instead, we lose our hope when we listen to the wrong internal voice. One of these voices is called shame. We admit that we are wretched without him, but we hide because we are afraid of God. We forget that he still wants to come close to us. He demonstrated this in the garden of Eden.

In the Genesis creation story, God said everything was good. Everything. Even the God-given freedom to choose whether to eat fruit from the forbidden tree was good. Adam and Eve walked with God personally. I imagine them joking with God and talking about the wonders of the universe under the starry sky. If I were Adam, I would've asked God to go fishing or on a run. He could teach me a thing or two about how to snorkel with sea turtles and great white sharks. Why not? With God there, I would be OK. It sounds perfect to be side by side with God on a regular basis.

Unfortunately, God, Adam, and Eve weren't the only ones in the garden. Evidently, Lucifer, an archangel removed from heaven due to his pride and iniquity (Luke 10:18), was also there and listening. Genesis 3:1 says, "Now the serpent was more crafty than any other beast of the field that the LORD God had made." The word *other* is not in the Hebrew Bible. He isn't the craftiest animal. He is a being like no other animal.

If I were the devil and I wanted to corrupt God's purpose and creation, I would think long and hard about my strategy. After all, God is all-knowing, all-powerful, and sees everything because he is everywhere. What the serpent does is revealing. It exposes where hopelessness begins.

In Genesis 2, God instructs the man what to do with the tree of knowledge. But in Genesis 3, all the serpent does is ask a question.

And just like that, knowing good and evil became as desirable to Adam and Eve as knowing God. Knowledge and information have a part to play and are important in our lives (Hosea 4:6); however, it must be the *right* knowledge and information. This is how hope interrupts the diatribe of hopelessness: Hopelessness speaks only lies.

Hopelessness never partners with God. God designed humanity to start with him as the source for truth and reality. Unfortunately, Eve didn't go to God. She said the serpent deceived her. But technically, she may have deceived herself. When she quoted God's rule to the serpent, she adds that God said "don't *touch* it" (Gen. 3:3 CEB, emphasis added). Or possibly the man failed to adequately pass on to the woman what God shared with him. If this occurred, Eve fell prey to Adam's mistake.

What we do know is that something happened between what God said in Genesis 2:16–17 and the moment they ate the forbidden fruit. A craving to know and understand, apart from believing and acting on what God says, always results in self-deception.

To corrupt God's purpose, the serpent's first and foremost assault was on God's identity. "Did God actually say?" (3:1). An attack on what God says is an attack on who God is (John 1:1, 14). The identity of humanity was next.

In Genesis 3:5, the serpent cunningly says, "You will be like God." Although the first humans were not divine, they were already like him—created in God's image. In other words, the serpent says, "God isn't who he says he is, and you are not who God says you are."

After Adam and Eve ate the fruit, they "knew that they were naked." Notice that the man and woman didn't become naked after they ate the fruit. They were always naked. But after they ate the fruit, they became ashamed of their nakedness.

In verse 8, they "heard the sound of the LORD God walking in the garden." They knew his voice and knew the sound of his walk. This tells me the first man and woman, Adam and Eve, didn't know God just from a distance. They even knew the difference between one of God's steps and that of a giraffe, lion, or Bengal tiger. Adam and Eve knew what God's feet sounded like when pressed against the dirt, the very dirt God had scooped up and breathed into to create humanity. And yet, even knowing God's kindness, they did something unthinkable. They hid.

The Unthinkable

We do strange things when we don't know what else to do. Years ago, we added a Goldendoodle to our family who now weighs seventy pounds. We live in a neighborhood where joggers tie their dog leash around their waist and go for runs. It always seems to work out well for them. I tried it. Once. Fig's large body jerked me within the first ten seconds of our run together because he wanted to chase a car. I threw my back out and limped back home. He's a great dog, but I still go on runs alone. After a few years with him, we added a second dog to our home. A mini Goldendoodle named Clover.

Fig trained Clover on dog etiquette. She sits, sleeps, and even chews treats the same way he does. Sometimes, though, she doesn't like to come inside after the final bathroom break before bedtime. We've tried everything. We stand at the door with treats. We tap the lid of her treat jar to attract her. We use Clover's first and middle name to get her to come, and somehow the sound of "Clover Jane" works for my wife—but not me.

A moment of sheer brilliance (or absurdity) flooded our home one evening when Clover refused to come inside.

Some of my favorite movies to watch are the Rocky and Creed franchises. The training, emotional ups and downs, and last bell ring always pull me in. One night when we couldn't get Clover to come and with the encouragement of my family I cried out "Yo, Adrian!" in my Rocky Balboa voice. Well, it worked. Our dog came running into the house immediately! I'm sure the neighbors think I'm crazy. Whether we want our dog to come inside or something more significant, we can get desperate. Rather like Adam and Eve.

Picture it: Adam and Eve have eaten the forbidden fruit. Spiritual poverty is their new reality. Sin and hopelessness have entered the world. Sin is any action, thought, word, or motive that is incongruent with the love, truth, and character of God. It can be something we do that violates God's heart, something we don't do that we should have, or a thought. Children are diagnosed with leukemia because Adam and Eve ate the fruit. Poverty exists because of that moment in the garden. Abuse, betrayal, depression, addiction, crime, suicide—all the awful events in our world are because Adam and Eve listened to the wrong voice.

Naked and now ashamed, their solution is much more foolish than my antics to get Clover in the house. They hide from God.

How ridiculous! No one can hide from God. God sees them just like he saw Hagar. Walking toward them, he asks, "Where are you?" (Gen. 3:9). God hasn't lost them. God isn't trying to narrow down their location. His question is more for them than for him. They forfeited who they were, severing connection with God, and those designed to be face-to-face with him are now cowering in the bushes.

But notice God didn't say, "How dare you! Because you ate the fruit, wars will ravage communities." Nor did God shout, "Because of your decision, fear and anxiety will run rampant." To be clear, God did not turn a blind eye to their decision. He told them the truth and held them accountable. He deals with the serpent and then foreshadows the life/death/resurrection of Jesus. Love doesn't tolerate that which destroys. Love is kind but it isn't fickle. God did not change his standards because of Adam and Eve's behavior. God is merciful and gracious, and he is also holy and true.

God's initial response when he finds them hiding is intentional, calculated, and telling. He asks, "Who told you that you were naked?" (v. 11). While God does confront them and they do experience the consequences of their decision, his priority in that initial moment is to confront the hopelessness and shame that settled into their lives when they listened to the wrong voice. In essence, God says, "First things first. That wasn't my voice. Why did you believe it?"

Like Adam and Eve, and like the Laodiceans, we are often destitute and lost in our spiritual poverty. We all have a tendency to either deny and ignore or be ashamed. In any scenario, God comes to us. That is the moment when the most important choice we will ever make starts to unfold.

Will you dare to believe what God says when he mercifully draws near? Will you respond to the knock at the door? Will you come out of hiding and let God clothe you and cover your shame? When you do, it is 100 percent guaranteed: God is even better than you ever imagined.

3

WHAT IS GOD LIKE?

Hope is the fruit of knowing God's character and how he really feels about us. But finding it requires us to overcome the discomfort that often accompanies being vulnerable before God. We must refuse to hide like Adam and Eve, stop pretending like the church in Laodicea, and embrace what God is truly like. Hopelessness is not ultimately a social construct or an emotional roadblock. It is believing the wrong voice about our current circumstance. Hebrews 10:23 says, "Let's hold on to the confession of our hope without wavering, because the one who made the promises is reliable" (CEB).

Hope seems and feels unreasonable—even irrational—at times. But our hearts can deceive us (Jer. 17:9). We shouldn't always believe everything we think or feel. There are ways of thinking that may seem normal and have lasted over time, but that doesn't make them ideal. For example, in the year 1700, maps still showed the state of California as an island. We all know the map is inaccurate because not one of us has been to the island of California. Likewise, the mapped experiences of your life may say hope is a fairy tale, but the truth is that your experience is not the end of the story.

Although hope and hopelessness are divergent, they are not competitive. Hope is powerful when, like Rahab's rope, it is tethered to our all-seeing, fully capable Father in heaven. It becomes a symbol of a soon-coming reality.

Hopelessness exists to divert your attention away from God's preferred future, locking your perspective on your situation. Do you need to let go of some things that have robbed you of hope? Are you at a place where you're ready to vulnerably tell God where you really are and let him meet you there? Do you war against yourself because you feel unworthy of God meeting you where you are? Do you feel as though God is disappointed in you or that God forgot about you? We hold on to hope, that tightly woven cord, because it gets us from where we are to where God is bringing us. The fact that you know something in your life is missing, a promise unseen, is an invitation by God to dare to hope again. You were designed for hope in God to become a lifestyle. You can get there. Psalm 71:14 can describe your life one day: "I will hope continually."

Don't give any place in your soul for the enemies of hope to convince you otherwise. The misleading narrative of our day is that things can't and won't change. So many believe the greatest moments of their lives are behind them. This way of thinking is being interrupted by the truth that thunders in Romans 8:24–25: "We were saved in hope. If we see what we hope for, that isn't hope. Who hopes for what they already see? But if we hope for what we don't see, we wait for it with patience" (CEB). Hoping in God will never disappoint you because "hope does not put us to shame" (5:5). Hope works because of who God is and what God does.

Believe It or Not

I like to read. I really like to see what I read. What do I mean? When I'm on a plane and I'm headed home after a long international flight, there is nothing better than opening a text from my wife or kids and seeing a few red hearts or smiley faces. Of course, what they write matters, but a random GIF, emoji, meme, or Memoji attached to the text makes it even better. We spend as much time making sure those who read our posts, our texts, even our emails, see what we are saying as much as they understand what we are trying to say.

The Hebrew blessing recorded in Numbers 6:22–27 was also intended not only to be read and spoken but also seen. Unfortunately, the imagery behind the Hebrew wording is lost. It's worth the investment to slow down and embrace these verses for what they are. You will see what God is like in a fresh and new way—reframing the possibilities in front of you.

> And the LORD spoke to Moses, saying: "Speak to Aaron and his sons, saying, 'This is the way you shall bless the children of Israel. Say to them:
> "The LORD bless you and keep you;
> The LORD make His face shine upon you,
> And be gracious to you;
> The LORD lift up His countenance upon you,
> And give you peace."'
> "So they shall put My name on the children of Israel, and I will bless them." (NKJV)

Let's unpack what is missing in our understanding. The first misunderstanding is about what's happening outside of the words. This prayer was only to be prayed corporately, by the high priest, over the people. The high priest wasn't just anyone. He was to be from the tribe of Levi. Only two priests were chosen in all of history based on merit: Aaron and Phinehas. When the time came for this rare priest to speak the blessing from the *Shaddai*[1] (the Hebrew word for "Almighty"), the priest held his hands up to form the letter *shin*, which looks like a W and is the letter for Shaddai. This moment when one man called down God's blessing was powerful, reverent, and only available periodically.

For those of us in Christ, we don't need a high priest to receive God's blessing. Jesus, who was not from the tribe of Levi but the tribe of Judah, is now our high priest. He intercedes for us in heaven (Rom. 8:34). What does he pray? Numbers 6 is an example of how Jesus prays over us as our high priest.

In addition, since we are now part of a royal priesthood (1 Pet. 2:9), we have the authority to pray this prayer over ourselves and our families as well. You could say this blessing represents our spiritual inheritance—God's blessing on our lives, his graciousness toward us, his radical kindness and overwhelming peace.

For the Israelites, the prayer was answered many times over the forty years in the desert. Amid countless struggles, uncertainties, and unpredictable challenges, the Israelites thrived. They had plenty of food and water, although there was no cold storage or formal agricultural education. They were protected from many enemies who tried to kill, rob, and enslave them.

After centuries of abuse and trauma, they learned how to live in families and raise children, looking toward the promise rather than backward, shackled to a painful past. Amid a drought-prone land, their flocks increased and had plenty to eat. Their children grew and were healthy in a time when routine medical care didn't exist.

They domesticated their lives and managed wealth even though they had been uneducated slaves with no frame of reference for thriving. The presence of God was tangible; literally, a ball of fire hovered in the sky outside their camp. They established a civil society with moral and civic laws far superior to all other cultures in their day. Even their shoes did not wear out although they walked countless miles under extreme weather conditions.

The prayer in Numbers 6 isn't necessarily just about what God does for us. It's about who God is. He is so loving and caring that our minds cannot comprehend it. Regardless of what language we speak, our words are always inferior and unable to capture the essence of his majesty. Ephesians 3:17–19 says Christ dwells within us so that we, "being rooted and grounded in love, may have strength to comprehend with all the saints what is the breadth and length and height and depth, and to know the love of Christ that surpasses knowledge, that [we] may be filled with all the fullness of God." God's love surpasses knowledge. And yet God invites us to pursue what is unknowable.

Our ability and willingness to live with two seemingly opposing truths often determines the effectiveness of our hope. One truth reveals how real our current situation is, but the superior truth underscores the character of God. A situation may contradict God's promise. We acknowledge this reality without bowing to it. Unwavering hope in God can coexist with where we currently are on our journey. We are not naive to situations that seem beyond hope. Neither do we allow them to change our view of God. This is how we trust God even when our experience seems to give us reasons not to.

The Character of God

The ancient Hebrew blessing in Numbers 6 begins with God (v. 24). It is about him—not us. But God doesn't like to do things without us. In your Bible, God's name may be written as either "Lord" or "Lord." Modern Bible versions use Lord when they translate the Hebrew word *Adonai*.[2] When they use Lord, it is translating another of God's names—*YHWH*[3] (as in Yahweh or Jehovah). YHWH is known as the ineffable name because he is so holy that early Israelites would never speak his name out loud. Don't ever lose the awe of being able to talk to God personally, by name.

When you meet a dignitary or someone of significant social stature, you are often taught to bow your head or demonstrate reverence. One time I met a tribal leader in western Africa. Cameras were not allowed in the hut. I was instructed not to speak to him unless first addressed. When I walked into the small room, he was surrounded by people who wouldn't look him in the eye and kept their heads bowed low. I was told to do the same.

God the Father is different. He doesn't want to criticize you, scold you, or lather divine disappointment all over you. No, God wants to bless you.

The English word "bless" is *barakh*[4] in Hebrew. It is in the piel form and means to bow down and present a gift to someone. When we come before the King of all kings, rather than expecting us to bow in reverence or, more accurately, humiliation due to the condition of our hearts, God does something unfathomable.

The imagery in the blessing is that God gets up off his throne, approaches us, and begins to bless us by bowing down in front of us. This is not because we are in any way superior to God. It is an example of hospitality still experienced to this day when a sheikh greets the honored guest at the door by bowing. God serves us with gifts such as mercy, grace, salvation, and love. It feels uncomfortable to think of God kneeling in front of us. The one who spoke everything into existence bows before those for whom Jesus was sent to die. Even if we've looked the King of Kings in the face and rejected him in the past, even if our lives were shaped by our own selfish desires, sabotaged by our shameful past, or paralyzed with hopelessness, God gets up to bless us. That's only the beginning. The word for "keep" is *shamar*, meaning to "wall."[5] It's a reference to a nomadic animal herder taking thorns and thistles and building a wall around his animals in the open country to keep predators away.

In some parts of Africa, I've seen tribesmen do this. Before darkness settles over the great plains, they will encircle their animals this way. Imagine hyenas or lions walking around a wall of thorns peering at you and your livestock. The sheer force of the animals, should they decide to penetrate the makeshift wall of debris, would mean certain harm or death to you and your treasured herd. But the predators won't penetrate the thorns.

When God kneels in front of us like a father speaking to his toddler, he then wraps his arms around us. Like a wall of thorns, his embrace keeps us safe while our enemy "prowls around [us] like a roaring lion" (1 Pet. 5:8). God kneels, not to angrily glare at us or accuse us but to get close and hold us.

The Shining Faces of God

In Numbers 6:25, the Hebrew word for "face," *panim*,[6] is plural, giving the idea that the knowable/unknowable God has many emotions and a reassuring presence. I can imagine

God turning his forgiving face to the humbled and his assuring face to those facing uncertainty. His firm yet loving face is directed to those who open the door to deception, and his gaze invites them back into the light. His confident face shines toward those who are afraid. It's almost as if God's face can contain more than one expression at a time, depending on who is looking at him. Ancient Hebrews believed the greatest consequence of sin wasn't eternal punishment after death. Rather, the worst discipline possible was God's hidden face. Wow. I don't know about you, but I think this should reawaken the privilege of prayer.

It is one thing for a holy God to turn his face toward us, inviting us into a relationship. But Scripture also says his face *shines* toward us. The same word used to describe what occurred in Genesis 1 when God separated light from darkness is used here. One Hebrew word is all it took for instantaneous combustion to occur in the cosmos during creation. Waves and particles coexist to compose light, the amazing substance revealing his face.

The shining face of God is a reminder that hopelessness is a trespasser. God still draws near today. Showing us his illuminated face is an intimate act that exposes all the things in our hearts. His face doesn't reflect what is happening within us or our world. It illuminates the truth of his promises available to us, fueling our hope. I feel as if I'm just now starting to understand this truth.

When God created humanity, he scooped up a mound of dirt and breathed life into it. It was before his face that we found our origin. I believe this is why so many of us struggle to find a resting place in our souls. We look for fulfillment in many places—wealth, relationships, being seen, pleasing our every desire. But we are never home until we behold his face. We are never at peace until we accept his invitation to know him and recognize his nearness on both the good and the bad days.

We were designed to live near him, close by, so that when he whispers, we hear him. We can keep getting closer and closer to him. Sometimes God doesn't speak but rather guides us, not with a word but with a glance.

When we see God's face, his graciousness is tangible. The word "gracious" (*chanan*)[7] means more than unmerited favor. It can also be translated as finding refuge, which in this context is found before God's shining face. God's grace isn't tolerant of compromise, nor does it excuse us from living in surrender. When we presume upon God's grace and live the way we prefer outside of God's design, we step out of God's presence and strip grace of the very power it wields. Vulnerability requires us to step into the light, where everything is exposed, and trust his arms will always wrap around us in protection. Grace isn't cheap. Yet it empowers us to reign in life.

As the graciousness of God begins to work and the blessing unfolds, my spiritual imagination runs wild. God gets ready to stand. Up to this moment, what we see YHWH do in Numbers 6:24–26 is stunning. The King of all kings knelt down in front of us as a sign of him welcoming us. He looked us right in the eyes and hugged us. Face-to-face, he picks us up. When God's countenance is lifted, it's because he lifts us up literally continuously.

It's like a grandparent who stoops down to embrace their grandchild. Once that occurs, we all know what happens next. The grandparent reaches out, picks up the little one, and stands. When a child is scooped up, they are often held above the face of the one who adores them. This is the word picture of what God does with us. He stands and lifts us up close to his shining face. When a young child is held high, their gaze always turns downward to the one who loves them.

This is where the peace of God becomes real. In this place of being closely held and with his shining attention, God grants us his peace, or *shalom*.[8] Literally, he prepares a table, a feast, a setting of shalom. Shalom is probably one of the more complex, indefinable words in Scripture. The peace God gives is more than emotional equilibrium. It is total completeness—spirit, soul, and body. Peace is the literal fulfillment of his kingdom come and will be done here and now—just like it will be then and there in heaven. Shalom embodies what it is like to leave our spiritual poverty and walk in our spiritual inheritance. This form of all-consuming peace is a result of seeing every experience in life pale in comparison to his expression.

God's shining face exposes everything for two main reasons: to lay it all down so his grace and mercy can cover it and to lift our eyes to where only hope will lead us—him. He lifts us higher than we can ever reach on our own. He smiles radiantly at us. Though we have nothing to offer God and can't possibly "buy gold refined in the fire" for him, he loves us (Rev. 3:18). This is why hope in God never puts us to shame (Rom. 5:5). Choose to know the unknowable.

I Am a Child of God

There is one more truth in the blessing of Numbers 6 that sticks out. It opens our eyes to the responsibility we have to bring hope to others. "The LORD spoke to Moses, saying: 'Speak to Aaron and his sons, saying, "This is the way you shall bless the children of Israel"'" (vv. 22–23 NKJV). Why didn't God speak all the hope he had in mind directly to the

Israelites? Because God designed us for one another. He often speaks the message of hope to us through others.

When our spiritual poverty becomes normal, not only does our spiritual inheritance go unclaimed; others also miss out on what it is like for God to bless them through us. In verse 22, God speaks to Moses and instructs him to speak to Aaron. Aaron, in turn, is supposed to share with others. This is how the blessing would overtake an entire nation.

What if Moses ignored God's voice? Or what if he chose to listen to the wrong voice? This blessing came to Moses during a very difficult time in his life and his nation's history. Despite the many obstacles he faced, Moses embraced who God was. Aaron and the others did too. There is a compound effect when one child of God after another dares to believe the truth about God's character.

As a young child, Mary tragically lost her mother. When someone told her something untrue and awful about God, she believed it. They said, "Mary, God does not love you."

Shortly after the death of her mother, due to civil war in her country, she remained at home with her other siblings while her father went off to fight. News reached Mary and the family of her father's death, and Maria was handed off to others to raise.

Abuse was common—even expected. Harsh words turned into physical beatings. Emotional and sexual abuse followed. As a young adolescent girl, she left and got married, hoping for a better life. Unfortunately, the home she left was better than the one with her husband.

Traumatized by the war, her husband became an abusive alcoholic. In desperation, after a horrific moment, she fled to another country to give her children a better life. But there was no better life there either. To feed her children, she chose to become a prostitute.

For over a decade, she entered one abusive relationship after another. She kept her job a secret from her children for as long as she could. She felt trapped with no other options. Mary described that time as being in the middle of a black hole where she couldn't see light anymore. She didn't think she deserved anything better. But God saw her like he did Hagar.

One day, a woman who was walking in the red-light district stopped and talked with Mary. The stranger had on clean clothes, smiled, and looked her in the eyes. This stranger befriended Mary and began speaking with her regularly. Mary dreamed of having clean clothes and a reason to smile too. One day, Mary experienced what she called "the light of God."

When I asked her what it felt like, she said, "It was like someone turned on the lights and I saw a way out. I realized that I too was one of God's children."

Where did the light of God come from? God's shining face found in the person who became Mary's friend, just as Moses spoke hope to Aaron who, in turn, modeled the same for others.

Now, Mary's life is transformed. She has a close relationship with God, owns her own business, and frequently goes to the red-light district to share how much God loves the other women.

Is God asking you to step out, like Mary or that stranger, and become a vessel for hope to flow through? Once you have caught a glimpse of God's shining face in your discouragement and hopelessness, you will never want to remain silent. He intends for you to turn toward others with compassion.

The lukewarm Christian lifestyle must end once and for all. Hopelessness stops today. Adopting a new normal and living out your unique, handcrafted purpose from God will bring hope to others as they also discover the God who greets them at the door with overwhelming hospitality. You are designed to live face-to-face with God, and your spiritual inheritance is waiting to be claimed—and then given away. There are others who need hope to defeat their impossibilities. God is ready to bless and keep them and to cause his face to shine in their direction too. But he needs you to say yes, just as Moses, Aaron, and others did. Flourishing in your life with God doesn't require obstacles being removed or changes in your situation. It can begin now.

4

CHANGE ME FIRST

I wandered through densely populated Southeast Asian streets in what is arguably one of the most hopeless places on earth. No one just happens to drive through this area. These people deserve to be remembered, and they also deserve our advocacy. They are seen, known, and adored by God, though most of them do not know it. The children I met are the third or fourth generation in their family to live in that particular area. It was at the very beginning of my joining the team at Convoy of Hope. I had no idea how much this moment would change me.

Stories like the one I am sharing are portrayed in movies and documentaries and are increasingly known through media. In this, lays a fear of mine: that we will become desensitized to the pain of others. We cannot allow the deep oceans of hopelessness to intimidate us or lull us to sleep. Familiarity can dim the light that once burned brightly. Perhaps the greatest enemy to hope is not hatred, inequality, extreme poverty, genocide, or atrocity; it is doing nothing.

Everyone I saw was eerily thin. Grown men looked just eight or nine years old due to malnutrition, and an unusually large amount of people were disabled in some way. An endless procession of people walked along the road through open sewage, carrying automobile-size bundles of plastic scraps. They were going to a facility miles away. Foraged trash was recycled in exchange for enough money to buy a small portion of rice. This kept the families alive for a few more days.

Most of the children had no shoes, wore torn and scant clothing, and were covered with a mixture of dirt, feces, and sores. They smelled of urine and likely housed parasites. I saw what hopelessness, in its primal form, looks like. You could see it in their eyes. I never saw one of the children smile. For them, drudgery and desperation were normal.

One day I watched as children formed a line stretching four city blocks long. A rusty truck slowly backed up to them with a few men standing in the back of the truck.

Men scooped rice out of the truck bed and placed it in the little hands. However, the children, who were incredibly malnourished and hungry, didn't automatically begin to eat. I was very surprised by this. When someone is severely hungry and they are given food, they usually don't wait to eat. Primal human instinct kicks in. But one of my local coworkers told me that he had followed some of the children back to the slums and watched as they shared the handful of rice with their little siblings. In this, I learned what sacrificial love really looks like.

In that moment of deep personal conviction, empathy, and sheer trauma from what I heard and saw, rain began to fall. In the torrential downpour, a stranger ran up to me and held up an umbrella. He wanted to shield me from becoming drenched. I watched the children protect the rice, keeping it from slipping through their fingers one grain at a time.

I politely thanked the individual for their kindness but asked for the umbrella to be put away. As I turned to him, I noticed in the distance a beautiful, ornately carved wooden door. It seemed ancient. In front of it stood little girls I estimated to be eight to ten years of age. Their dressy clothing was vibrant and colorful, arraying them in various shades of pink and purple, and they wore bright lipstick. It brought back a memory of my two daughters when they were very young.

Fridays were my day with the girls. After eating Dad's pancakes for breakfast, they played tea party, dance party, dress-up, and my favorite, wedding day, where I pretended to officiate their weddings. The girls have been married a few hundred times!

After my memory faded, I said to the gentleman traveling with me, "Oh look, even here the little girls are playing dress-up."

He responded, "Heath, those precious girls are not playing dress-up. That door belongs to the brothel. Here, little girls their age are abducted and sold. Most will die of AIDS and never be free."

I was overwhelmed with anger at the injustice. Surrounded by children who were beautiful and worth so much more, I felt helpless. I then realized that how I felt was nothing in comparison to how each child around me must have felt. They deserved to know there was a world in which they could be tucked in bed at night, provided for, prayed with, and protected. I wanted to see all of the hungry children experience an end to the poverty that burdened their families for generations.

I cried and stood in the rain a long time. I clenched my jaw and talked to God. As we made our way through the neighborhood, the rain subsided, the line of children faded, and the view of the brothel disappeared. Approximately twenty minutes later, we stepped into a building full of laughter and singing. It was one of the most jarring and beautiful moments of my life.

Something Was Different

Inside the building, little girls with pigtails held hands and twirled in circles. They had life in their eyes, and I saw the first smiles of the day. The contrast of the joy I saw there and the deep despair I saw on the streets was impossible to reconcile. A bell rang and children ran from all directions toward the tables situated in the center of the room. Each child seemed to know where to sit. Someone gave thanks to God for the food, and then the children began to eat a hot, nutritious meal filled with meat, vegetables, and rice. I watched as they giggled and talked. It was a completely different world. When I spoke with some of the children, I could see the light in their eyes. Even in deep, deep darkness, a light can shine.

Of course, darkness doesn't really exist inasmuch as the absence of light does. But in that dark place, God's light came, and hope was born through something as practical as a plate of nutritious food and clean, pure water. It doesn't take much to give someone hope. We just have to see God at work in the rubble.

The difference between the children in the building and those on the streets has nothing to do with where they live or how educated their parents are. They all live in the same place and have parents who pick up plastic. They all sleep on dirt floors. For generations, society has told these beautiful people that the gods placed them on the earth to suffer. Dreaming of a better day or starting a new beginning isn't an option when you believe the gods destined you to a life like this. Many listened to the wrong voice just as Adam and Eve did in the garden. They didn't know any better. No one had ever told them the truth. Like you and me, they are created in God's image, and he longs to turn his shining face toward them as well.

The significant difference between the children in the building and those on the streets comes down to one thing: hope. Though their surroundings were almost identical, not all of them saw the same thing. Hope may not change *what* we see, but it does change *how* we see.

Once we see through hope's lens, it is almost impossible to unsee. Choosing to ignore the truth will never change anything. We must vulnerably and courageously acknowledge the way things are while refusing to be redefined by them. I saw firsthand on those streets how hope changes us much more than it changes our circumstances.

We used to be wretched, poor, blind, and naked. Some of us lacked self-awareness, denying the truth and claiming to be anything but spiritually poor. Others fell prey to the lie of self-dependency. Tragically, some hid in shame. Regardless of our stories, we had a spiritual inheritance left unclaimed. Then there was a knock at the door. For some of us, it happened years ago, and we just need to be reminded that God is still with us. Perhaps for you, the knock occurred while reading this book, and you bent your heart in God's direction and surrendered all to him. You opened the door to God, and hope walked in.

Despite your circumstances, you're now seated at a table with him. You live in the same situation you did a moment ago, but like the amazing children who dance and sing, you see something different. It's as if the bush that was on fire finally caught your attention. The God who hospitably bows, who lovingly picks you up like a tender father, directs his gaze toward you. His face shines. You catch a fresh glimpse of who he truly is and how he really feels about you. Now, you have not only an opportunity but also a responsibility. The next step is up to you.

Isaiah Sees God

One of the most peculiar stories in Scripture is in Isaiah 6. But before we jump into the story, let's set the scene. Isaiah grew up during a time of national prosperity and had access to influential leaders like King Uzziah of Judea. Initially, Uzziah was highly successful. He fortified his nation against foreign invaders and organized a strong army. His soldiers were equipped with the most sophisticated weapons of the day. He conquered lands and took them from the Arabians and Philistines. Even the Ammonites, an enemy of Israel for centuries, paid tribute.

Uzziah valued innovation and technology. He used these to strengthen his military, and he developed infrastructure and water access points all around Judea. The wells made animal husbandry and herding strong economic enterprises. Vineyards flourished. Life was good.

But at the height of his success, Uzziah became casual in his relationship with God. He tried to offer incense in the temple, a service reserved exclusively for descendants of Aaron. He was immediately struck with leprosy, which in this story, serves also as a metaphor for what spiritual compromise will do. The king lived in quarantine for the rest of his life.

When Uzziah died, national stability and the certainty of Isaiah's future were unknown. Things appeared fragile. It takes great humility to be vulnerable before God when it is just plain hard. I think it is less about whether we think we need the nearness of God and more about our fear of being completely vulnerable to God. We doubt our worthiness.

This is the scenario behind the moment when heaven and earth collide and the prophet Isaiah sees God and angelic beings surrounding God's throne. Isaiah is awestruck and describes everything in meticulous detail.

Three Times

What does God look like? Isaiah doesn't describe his features. He does describe God's posture and surrounding activity. God is seated on a throne higher than others. The earthly king was gone but the real throne was not empty. God, who presides over everything in this life, is still there, sitting down, as he rules. In Isaiah 6:1, Isaiah refers to God as *Adonai* meaning "my great Lord." This was a term used for kings.[1] God is not pacing frantically, nor is he nervous. During a time of national crisis, God is at rest and enthroned. This is important to remember.

When rioters take to the streets, elections divide communities, national legal proceedings swarm, relationships are fractured, or anxiety convincingly approaches you again, God is still seated. Grocery bills may rise and global instability may increase, but God has not abdicated his throne. In Acts 7, just before Stephen is martyred, he sees "Jesus standing at the right hand of God" (v. 55). Scripture says God stood up. Jesus stoops to bless us and hospitably welcome us, but he stands to his feet when we are treated unjustly. God the Father is fully at peace and seated as he reigns.

Isaiah also noticed the train of God's robe. When a bride walks down the aisle, her train follows her. The moment she stops walking, the train stops moving. Isaiah saw a different phenomenon: "the train of [God's] robe filled the temple" (Isa. 6:2). In Hebrew, the idea is "the train of his robe filled and filled and filled and filled the temple."[2] God was seated, but the train of his royal regalia was still moving. At this time in history, a valiant king's army stripped the jewels off the crown of the defeated king. Those jewels were then sewn on the robe of the victorious king while the defeated leader, if they survived, was paraded through the streets to shame them. Isaiah saw God as the always victorious king he is. His train isn't just long. It never stops. Isaiah and all of heaven were in awe.

The angels cried out to one another. What are they saying? "Holy, holy, holy!" (v. 3). We are not the topic of heavenly conversation; God is. The angels are consumed with God's holiness and God's glory. Holiness means infinite, unique, distinct, of the highest quality and therefore unimaginable. It also means beautiful brilliance.

In Hebrew, when emphasis is being placed on something, the word is doubled. For example, if we grab a cup of espresso together, and I really like it, I would say, "This espresso is 'good-good.'" That slice of cheesecake would be "delicious-delicious." The newborn baby is "cute-cute."

But God is not "holy-holy"; he is "holy, holy, holy." The angels used the same word three times. Nowhere in ancient Hebrew is a word tripled except when referring to God's holiness.

Isaiah saw national disparity and economic uncertainty. He was grieving the loss of a king who did many things well but failed at the most important thing. Amid all this, what the angels saw and how they saw it was different. Just as the children in the slums saw the same scenario but through different eyes, the angels acknowledged that the earth is full of the weighty presence of God.

For the discouraged mom who is lying awake at night, the glory of God is there. The very moment another medical bill arrives in the mail and you realize there isn't enough money to pay it, God's glory is there. In the middle of a warzone where children are vulnerable, God is there. The presence of external situations contrary to God's character are not indicative of God's absence. God is always there. God is always here. As God reveals his holiness, the foundations shake (v. 4). According to Hebrews 12:27, one day everything that can be shaken will be. This is why we tether the cord of hope to God and not to a bank account, job, network, or our own abilities. God's kingdom will never be shaken (v. 28). When we pray, we lend our voice to something unshakable.

Brokenness and Confession

In response to God's overwhelming holiness, Isaiah realizes that what used to overwhelm and discourage him is no longer of consequence. Isaiah is hopelessly ruined and undone as, in the very presence of God, his spiritual poverty is revealed. He cries out to God in agony and confesses the truth about who he really is. He doesn't blame anyone; he has no excuse to make.

Instead, Isaiah says, "Woe is me!" (Isa. 6:5). Old Testament prophets used the word *woe* to communicate very heavy news, such as an impending crisis. It can be likened to pronouncing a curse. Though he was used to saying, "Woe to this nation," Isaiah doesn't blame Uzziah for the hopeless situation he is in. He makes the right choice when he acknowledges his spiritual poverty. His first response to God's holiness and glory is utter humility.

Humility is not passive; it is active. Isaiah was not being insecure. He was appropriately responding by saying "woe is me." When humility is absent, God's presence almost always is too.

Rather than referring to God as Adonai, as he did earlier in his experience, the text says he now refers to God as YHWH (Yahweh). His understanding of who God is changes. It isn't that Isaiah didn't know God personally before, but he now catches a fresh glimpse of the God who never changes.

Isaiah notices that his lips are "unclean," a ceremonial term that basically means unholy. As a prophet, he fulfilled his calling by speaking on behalf of God. The very thing that paid his bills, that would have created a sense of earthly significance, is now embarrassingly repulsive compared to God. His very best doesn't even come close to the God who is holy, holy, holy. He realizes, as we all must, that he is spiritually poor while living in a culture of abundance. He is broken, and he knows it. In his surrender, something occurs in his heart that creates an environment for hope to flourish. Surrendering is something we all can and must do if we want to take hold of our spiritual inheritance.

Being broken is different from living in brokenness. We are broken when we hide from God. We are broken when we live in denial. We are broken when we try to meet the most primal of human needs through materialism. Or when we react to our circumstances by becoming oppressors, abusing power, and taking advantage of the marginalized. The insecure and ashamed become ensnared by the all-too-convincing lies the accuser tells. The proud are consumed by the insatiable appetite of hopelessness, refusing to live vulnerably with God, often out of self-preservation and fear. We are broken when we choose to ignore God and are impressed with ourselves instead.

However, when we humble ourselves and admit the broken state we are in, God has something to work with. Ernest

Hemingway put it this way: "The world breaks everyone and afterwards many are strong at the broken places."[3] Brokenness is a heart posture, like Isaiah's humble acknowledgement of the chasm between God's holiness and his own condition. It is a result not of fixating on where we are in comparison to God's best but only on the awe and wonder of our God who personally and deeply loves us anyway. Brokenness positions us to live with a constant reminder of how far God has brought us and how far he will take us. Brokenness causes God to draw near (Ps. 34:18) and to heal the brokenhearted (147:3). To make us whole, God sent his Son to die for everyone who is broken.

Once Isaiah acknowledges his spiritual condition in Isaiah 6:5, an angel takes a hot coal from the altar and touches his lips. What seems like a strange reaction to Isaiah's proclamation is actually God's way of revealing truth to Isaiah in a way he would understand. The nations around Judea at this time used altars for religious sacrifices. Hot coals or stones heated the sacrifice to appease the gods and goddesses. The fire touched the sacrifice. Through touching Isaiah's lips with a hot coal, God is revealing to him that his life is the sacrifice God desires—not as a human sacrifice but as a living one. Isaiah admits he is broken, and in this state of brokenness rather than pride or denial, he finds healing.

The coal is a symbol of how Isaiah's guilt is taken care of—it is through sacrifice. The coals from the altar point toward what God will ultimately do for us all by sending his Son into the world (John 3:16–17). Once Isaiah confesses, God absolves his guilt. Confession comes first. It is important to see this sequence.

The gospel is how God takes our broken lives and restores us. This sheer act of grace and mercy on God's part is the only way we can each have a relationship with him. When we confess our brokenness, God makes good on his promise to heal our hearts.

Personally, I still have a long way to go in this area. I won't make any excuses. But I'm committed to living and growing in brokenness before God all the days of my life. He deserves it all.

Back to the story in Isaiah 6. There is now an abrupt scene change, and our eyes are turned back onto God. While Isaiah is processing his experience of seeing God, hearing the angels praise God's holiness and glory, and watching a fiery coal come straight toward his lips, God is having a conversation. There is always a conversation going on in heaven that we are often unaware of. I'm reminded of the time when Jacob said, "Surely the LORD is in this place, and I did not know it" (Gen. 28:16). Whatever you need to do, get to that place where God draws near to you. Know that place, the place of God.

God asks those around him whom they can send to earth on their behalf. Isaiah responds quickly, volunteering to go back and do what he did before. But this time, it will be different. Isaiah's collision with the reality of God doesn't change what he is going through personally or nationally. However, after catching a fresh glimpse of God, that is the last thing on his mind. Isaiah now wants God to do a deep work in him first. This one thing changes everything. For the rest of his life, Isaiah will never unsee his glimpses of heaven. And I will never forget those children who taught me that hope doesn't change what you see, but it certainly changes how you see.

God in the Rafters

In the nineteenth century, the island of Zanzibar was a final stop before heading into the unending interior of Africa.

Merchants said goodbye to the harbor and the sea and ventured into territory full of danger. After months, even years, those who survived emerged from the mainland with ivory, exotic animals, gum, and gold. At the time, the vast island was the capital of the Omani Empire, a place where trade expansion across the Indian Ocean generated innumerable fortunes. The Sultan of Zanzibar, Sayyid Barghash bin Said, ruled authoritatively. Rumors of Zanzibar's strategic location and gateway to wealth spread across Europe. In 1893, Britain laid claim to the island, and it became a state of the British Empire until 1963.

Zanzibar was also an epicenter for the slave trade. From what is now known as Malawi, across to Uganda and the DRC, slave traders brought their soon-to-be-sold "property" to the island. By the 1850s, as many as seventy thousand slaves were held there. Opportunists who were numb to the value and dignity of each human being, made in God's image, gathered there to purchase slaves. Everyone profited from the slave trade except those who were sold. The treatment of slaves was horrific, but ending the practice was unthinkable to slave owners in that day. They used their slaves to fight wars and forced others to become concubines. Owners removed the people from their biological families and stole all their rights. Slaves who survived typically lived only a short time and in much suffering.[4]

William Wilberforce, an English politician, and David Livingstone, a Scottish missionary, were the two primary figures behind the long and tiresome campaign to abolish the Atlantic slave trade. Many in Livingstone's nation disdained him for boldly proclaiming truth against the injustice. Wilberforce tried repeatedly to end the slave trade. On February 18, 1796, his motion to abolish the trade would have carried by twenty-six votes, but it was delayed.

When it came time to vote, Wilberforce "complained that there were about a dozen supporters absent."[5] His motion was defeated, seventy-four votes to seventy. If the supporters had been present, they could have easily carried the vote. Where were the political leaders? They were at the opera.[6]

Had the politicians said yes, not to entertainment but to the dignity of each human being, who knows how many lives would have been spared. As you read this, is God inviting you to be courageous, to show up, and to say yes to what really matters? If so, do it. Heaven is asking who will go.

In 1834, England's parliament abolished the Atlantic slave trade. But it wasn't until several years later, on June 5, 1873, that the British government forced Sultan Barghash to end the trade and Zanzibar's slave market ended.[7] For Zanzibar, it was finally time to build toward the future.

A few years later, the Universities' Mission to Central Africa built Christ Church Cathedral in Zanzibar. Its altar sits directly above where the former whipping post stood. Known as the Slave Market Church, it was originally constructed using some of the beams and timber from the former slave trade's assets. The first service was held Christmas Day 1877. It is now part of a preservation project and is recognized as a World Heritage Site.

Freed slaves stood and found peace with God on the very ground where they and their loved ones were sold. I can imagine former slaves looking to the sky, trying to unravel years of traumatic and overwhelming brutality. They would look beyond the evidence of their indescribable struggle toward the face of God to pray and worship. Zanzibar was full of courageous people who were so transformed spiritually they could stare through a ceiling built over their past and lock eyes with God. This is what real hope deep within us all can look like.

Isaiah acknowledged his reality and the heartbreak associated with King Uzziah's life and death, but he still saw the Lord. The worshipers in Zanzibar see God too. Do you see God for who he truly is in your life right now? He is there with you.

Here I Am

In Isaiah 6, when God asks who they should send, he has something in particular on his mind and heart. Rather than sending an angel to accomplish his purpose or doing it himself, he is looking for someone like you and me to link arms with heaven. The architect who planned the church in Zanzibar didn't pray for God to miraculously build a cathedral out of former slave ships. No, people got to work, took apart the ships, and started to build. God is high, lifted up, and seated on his throne, but this truth can never become an excuse for complacency. Isaiah stepped up and said, "Here I am!" (v. 8) before his circumstances changed. The children in the slums choose to dance and sing even in the middle of extreme poverty. Hope is active. Like Isaiah, say, "Here I am," and shift your focus to what God is doing.

SECTION 2

SPIRITUAL INHERITANCE

5

THE EYES OF YOUR HEART

The Sahel is a region of land stretching across sub-Saharan Africa. Part of the western side of the Sahel is Burkina Faso. The first time I went to Burkina, I was struck by how much joy the villagers had. They lacked food and water, but they did not lack hospitality and kindness. You can learn a lot about humanity and God when the demonstration of love costs something. I have so, so much more growing to do as a follower of Jesus. The dust in the air and intense heat in Burkina are also things I will always remember. Due to a brief rainy season, farmers grow and yield their food within only a few months.

Celebration fills the air in October and November. With storehouses full of food, everyone is privileged with two meals per day. Villagers prepare meals with recipes and techniques passed down orally and visually over the centuries. Grains are turned to powder to create dough and something akin to porridge. It sits heavily in their stomachs, and the children sleep peacefully. Food preservation in this part of the world is just as important as animal husbandry and agriculture. To conserve their food, families will survive on one meal per day in February if they do not have other sources of food from animals. When this occurs, malnutrition sets in, nursing mothers struggle to keep their infants fed, and toddlers don't have the energy to play.

I once visited another remote area in Burkina Faso where a woman spends an average of four hours a day looking for water. She spends an additional two hours searching for firewood or fuel to boil the water to kill the parasites to keep her family alive. In the middle of the desert, we drove up to a water well. Women stood in line with their children at their sides. At the top of the well was a sign written in Arabic and another language. It stated that if the women would convert to a specific religion, they could draw water from the well. If they would not convert, they and their children would go thirsty. This is an injustice.

Water should never be weaponized to force conversions. Love for God is never mandated. There are many forms of oppression and evil all over the world. Each and every time I witness evil, I'm stunned at how much hopelessness there is as well as how darkness in the human heart often perpetuates it. People deserve better.

The Convoy of Hope team ended up installing another water well nearby. Anyone, regardless of age, gender, ethnicity, or creed, can draw water from that well.

The month of April is usually when the pain of hunger changes the sound of the desert. The wind still kicks up walls of dust hundreds of feet in the air. The heat still penetrates the skin and makes it hard to breathe. But the babies cry with minimal sound because they are just too weak.

Hanging in the corner of a hut where goats may be found or inside a granary is enough food to make the suffering and hopelessness go away. All someone needs to do is take down the grain, grind it into powder, and make porridge and dough again. The children would dance, the parents would rejoice, and hunger would fade. Unfortunately, that can't happen.

Why? It is the seed grain for the harvest to come. It is the only hope they have for their future. In May, if drought does not prevent the rainy season from coming, the men in the village will walk with the boys and throw the grain on the soil. It is a risk. Their hope in the harvest to come is proven by their faith in the withheld seeds.

Reason and Responsibility

There is a relationship between the condition of our souls (hearts) and the effectiveness of our spiritual journeys. Third John 2 says, "Beloved, I pray that all may go well with you and that you may be in good health, as it goes well with your soul."

For example, when we surrender to the reality of the gospel, we become new creations (2 Cor. 5:17). All things are brand new. And yet, we must still renew our minds (Rom. 12:1–2). Our spiritual inheritance in Christ is real and tangible. It points toward that day when we will spend an eternity with God, but it also starts now. This doesn't mean that as we grow spiritually and learn to abide in Jesus we experience some sort of amnesia. We still have memories, experiences, habits, relationships, and consequences in our lives that affect us. We ignore our pasts to the detriment of our souls and our spiritual journeys. We lay hold of the gift of salvation, a gift made possible only by grace (Eph. 2:8–9), yet we work out our salvation one choice at a time (Phil. 2:12). We are saved by grace, yet without works, our faith means nothing (James 2:26).

I'm learning more and more, after decades of walking with Jesus, that I haven't scratched the surface of who he is and what is already accessible through him. It reminds me of what T. S. Eliot says,

> We shall not cease from exploration
> And the end of all our exploring
> Will be to arrive where we started
> And know the place for the first time.[1]

In Ephesians 1, Paul reveals to us that we receive our spiritual inheritance both immediately, by grace, and as we grow, by faith. This inheritance made available to us should captivate our hearts. When it does, it changes how we live. You could put it this way: It is no longer enough to simply have hope. We must intimately know it in a way that moves our hope from being a possession to something we invest in. The greatest source of understanding and wisdom is not intellectual—it is spiritual. We do not merely think with the mind. We also think with the heart (Prov. 23:7).

What we know, therefore, is based not on intellectual facts alone but also on the facts and truths of who God is. Faith is "the assurance of things hoped for, the conviction of things not seen" (Heb. 11:1). We can't see everything God is doing on our own. This is why Paul teaches us to pair our hope with faith. We have a reason to hope; therefore, we have a reason to live by faith. With this also comes a responsibility to become who God designed us to be. The majority of what God can do within us and through us is the result of who we are becoming in him.

The burning bush was the starting line for Moses. He went back to the Egyptian palace where he grew up and partnered with God to liberate a few million Hebrew slaves from Egypt. The second half of Moses's life was full of miracles and heartbreaks. God parted the Red Sea when Moses stretched out his staff. God caused a river of water to flow from a rock, enough water to hydrate a few million people, when Moses obeyed. God provided food day after day in the hot desert where there was no cold storage or warehousing. When Moses was 120 years old, his eyesight was impeccable and his strength unweakened (Deut. 34:7). For all practical purposes, he could have continued for years to come. But though he saw the promised land from a distance, he never stepped foot into it. Instead, he stepped from this life to the next. The journey would continue with another leader.

Between finding our hope and receiving our inheritance, we will experience adversity. In the beginning of the book of Joshua, when Joshua takes over from Moses, God reaffirms the inheritance he'd promised Moses. He says, in essence, "Joshua, every place you step is part of what I'm giving you. But if you stop walking, you will forfeit what you already have." Joshua had a reason to move forward into the promise, and he did so.

A few chapters later, when the battle of Jericho is won, Rahab and her family survive, and she becomes part of the genealogy of Jesus. Her experience gives us the rich meaning of what it looks like to hope in who God is. God orchestrated many other miracles as well because Joshua not only had a reason for hope, but he also accepted the responsibility of faith.

Writing to a group of Christians in the ancient city of Ephesus, the apostle Paul explains the nature of our spiritual inheritance. But before doing so, he shares what he prays for them and why he prays for them.

First, Paul defines who he is writing to—a group of people he calls "saints" (Eph. 1:1). This is not a group of spiritual elites or ministers. God does not have different tiers of importance in his kingdom. Those Paul refers to are all Christians—both then and now. They, we, all have an inheritance because of Jesus (v. 11).

Then, Paul describes part of our spiritual inheritance, which includes receiving "every spiritual blessing" we could imagine (v. 3), being chosen or handpicked by God to know him (v. 4), and being adopted into his family (v. 5). We have been redeemed, or purchased back, by God. Think of that. God bought back something he created. We were already his, but he redeemed us again, forgiving us "according to the riches of his grace" (v. 7). Scripture mentions many other aspects of our inheritance both in Ephesians 1 and elsewhere. This is only the beginning. It will take all of eternity to unravel the extent of our inheritance.

As if that weren't enough, our indescribable inheritance comes with a guarantee. We "were sealed with the promised Holy Spirit, who is the guarantee of our inheritance until we acquire possession of it" (vv. 13–14).

After Paul describes our inheritance, he says he remembers all believers in his prayers, that God may "give [them] the Spirit of wisdom and revelation in the knowledge of him, having the eyes of [their] hearts enlightened, that [they] may know what is the hope to which he has called [them], what are the riches of his glorious inheritance in the saints" (vv. 17–18).

Paul longs for believers to truly see with the eyes of their hearts, like children who experience the joy of ice cream before they even take the first bite. The Spirit of God makes it possible for us to see beyond the ordinary, difficult, impossible, boring, or irrelevant and to lock eyes on a very real, tangible spiritual inheritance. The inheritance we have in God is both here and now and there and then.

Our inheritance includes eternal life with God after we die, when God reveals all things and sets them right. It also encompasses our lives today. Jesus asks us to pray for the kingdom to come and for God's will to be done on earth. Paul is eager for all Christians to know the *hope* and *inheritance* we have. And that's not all. He also reveals the relationship between hope and faith: Hope is part of our inheritance (v. 18), and we possess our inheritance by faith (v. 13).

When Gerald Cotton, thirty-year-old CEO of QuadrigaCX, suddenly and tragically passed away in 2018, those closest to him were left struggling to find answers. There were accusations of mishandling funds, and the details surrounding his death were a source of controversy.[2] As a leader of a digital exchange company, his untimely death heightened multiple legal and corporate complexities. Privacy and confidentiality were a competitive advantage for the company. The former CEO earned the trust of his partners due to their perception of his unwavering commitment to security. He'd said protecting the investments of his customers was top priority, and that is one of the reasons why people entrusted his company with hundreds of millions of dollars.

Multiple steps were methodically taken to avoid his then five-year-old business, sitting in the digital currency space, from being hacked. Unfortunately, the CEO's efforts were so secure that, after his passing from this life to the next, not one other person knew what the passwords were to access the inventoried cryptocurrency—more than $200 million worth to be exact. Courts, lawsuits, highly trained tech professionals, concerned investors, and employees dealing with uncertainty all collided. I am not fully sure, as of the date of this writing, what has or will happen to the inheritance that is locked away under password protection.

There is an inheritance for each one of us far more valuable than Cotton's cryptocurrency, and it is accessible. We don't need to sift through layers of spiritual coding or plead with God to receive it. Psalm 16:5 says God is our inheritance, and Ephesians 1 says we are his. It goes both ways. God, who is seated on his throne, paid the price for our inheritance by sending his Son. And we take hold of it through hope and faith.

One Step at a Time

As a cupbearer to a Persian king named Artaxerxes, Nehemiah had a peculiar job. He spent his days around the most powerful leader in the vast empire. He ate delicacies meal after meal and listened in on some of the most important conversations to ever take place with the king. There was only one catch: As cupbearer, his job was to test food meant for the king, ensuring that it wasn't poisoned. Knowing each meal may be his last probably took away some of the allure of dining with royalty. There are no public, measurable miracles recorded about Nehemiah—either in the book bearing his name or in other books. We have no record of an angel appearing to him. The path paved with miracles walked by people such as Moses, David, and Daniel didn't appear to be the same one Nehemiah walked. Miracles, however, are often shrouded in the difficult moments.

Unusual miracles occur every day through ordinary people. The discouraged person can walk right past or over them, oblivious to what God is doing.

But hope causes us to slow down long enough to really see. Nehemiah is a story about a royal waiter who received permission from his king to go to the land of his ancestors and begin a construction project. Nehemiah was trained in dinner etiquette. He was not an architect or engineer. His experience and ability wouldn't help him with what God had in store. But God doesn't see things the way we do.

Ancient Jerusalem was obliterated by the Babylonian army in the sixth century BC. Not only was the city destroyed but the spiritual climate of ancient Israel was too. The epicenter of spiritual life, Solomon's Temple, was leveled to the ground. Approximately 140 years afterward, Nehemiah heard about the social and spiritual rubble of Jerusalem. Many others no doubt heard the same. Everyone knew God would want the temple repaired. Few were willing to do anything about it. But Nehemiah said yes to what he knew God wanted. Most would dream of a life of luxury and proximity to influence, refusing to give up what Nehemiah did. His privileged life meant nothing to Nehemiah in light of God's greater purpose. Saying yes to God's best is always the right choice, no matter the cost.

Arriving in the devastated city of ancient Jerusalem, Nehemiah did something unique. In the middle of the night, he mounted his animal and went on a ride to inspect the damage (Neh. 2:12). It was dark and difficult to know what lay ahead. Taking a step of faith often requires walking in the dark. With God, we can still see.

The ruins were hard to traverse, preventing Nehemiah from taking the journey as planned (vv. 14–15). The ruins represented so many things to passersby: an homage to a past that felt better than the present, a reminder that God's promises can seem far away, a guarantee that making progress would be hard, and a constant reminder of the work needed to effect real change. But to Nehemiah, the rubble represented something different.

Then I [Nehemiah] said to them, "You see the trouble we are in, how Jerusalem lies in ruins with its gates burned. Come, let us build the wall of Jerusalem, that we may no longer suffer derision." And I told them of the hand of my God that had been upon me for good, and also of the words that the king had spoken to me. And they said, "Let us rise up and build." So they strengthened their hands for the good work. (vv. 17–18)

Notice the adjective used to describe the work. Though surrounded by ruins and trouble, Nehemiah knew that God's hand was upon him for good. The work, rather than being described as difficult, unbearable, frustrating, or wearisome, is described as "good." Nehemiah wasn't cavalier or naive. His hope-filled ambitions did not blind him to the obstacles. Hope acknowledges the size of the challenge at hand. It also acknowledges God is always greater.

Like Nehemiah's dream to rebuild the walls of Jerusalem, positive change is never an easy task. His story and ours will be full of obstacles.

One of the first obstacles Nehemiah faced was criticism. People around him described the work not as good but basically as impossible. "Will they revive the stones out of the heaps of rubbish?" (4:2). Perhaps there are voices in your life that create discouragement, doubt, or shame. Another step of faith you may have to take is to ignore some of those voices, though they may be familiar or sound convincing.

There were also moments of distress. Saying yes to the power of hope isn't a one-and-done commitment. It is a lifestyle. When it seemed like giving up was the only option, the Israelites said, "There is too much rubble" (v. 10). But Nehemiah didn't quit.

He was surrounded by cynicism (6:3–5). He even had advice given to him from a source that seemed reliable but, in the end, proved not to be (vv. 12–14). Most of all, Nehemiah didn't allow his self-talk, which is formative, to distract him from what mattered most. When we adopt negative attitudes and misplace our hope, it is usually a sign we've forgotten what is perhaps one of the most profound privileges we have in life: God stands with us in the ruins.

Decades of failed building projects and efforts came before Nehemiah. Others attempted to do what Nehemiah would eventually achieve. But he didn't allow a past history of failure to become predictive of what hope could do. He got to work.

Fifty-two days later, the wall around Jerusalem was rebuilt (v. 15).

A few years ago during a trip to Jerusalem, I saw an excavated section of Nehemiah's wall. It wasn't nearly as impressive as the other walls around me. The stones Nehemiah's crew used were jagged, varying in size, and seemed to be set in place more by accident than expertise. Yet the wall, after thousands of years of invasions and wars, still remains in some places.

Nehemiah's seemingly random ride during a sleepless night ended up becoming a miracle. Nehemiah had dismounted his animal and walked by faith, the evidence of things hoped for, even though his journey was surrounded by ruins.

Nehemiah didn't see rubble. He saw stones God had given him to build with. The farmers in the Sahel don't see the last of their food being tossed into the mud; they see a harvest to come. Moses saw a bush aflame with God when many others would have assumed it was merely an illusion.

Seeing beyond what others see is what it means to have "the eyes of your heart enlightened." When we see with the heart, our inheritance in God is more real than anything we can smell, taste, or touch.

To be clear, there is a place for the rational and natural in our faith walk. I can have faith all day long that I'm going to be a professional football player, but my size, skills, age, and genetics say otherwise. Much like hope, faith accepts reality without being limited by it. Hope in God is unshakable (2 Cor. 1:7) and bold (v. 3:12).

Say Yes to Trusting God

The very situations that are the sources of discouragement or hopelessness don't need to be changed before you take the next step with God. Nehemiah didn't wait for the sun to rise before he walked around the ruins. He was both willing and able to walk under the cover of darkness even though he was barely able to make out what was in front of him. It is no coincidence that the Hebrew Sabbath begins not at sunrise when light makes our path visible but at dusk. The best time to take a step of faith is when hope compels us to rely on God and remember that he is the precious inheritance we are pursuing.

When we realize God has given us minds to be renewed, we can turn to him and seek his wisdom. Also, he brings trustworthy people with God-honoring characters into our lives as sources of advice. And Scripture reveals the boundaries of what is pure, just, and good, and tells us how to think and live accordingly. We don't need to attempt to grow spiritually and renew our minds alone; however, we do have a choice to make that God and others cannot make for us. As he did with Joshua, God also asks you to be strong and courageous (Josh. 1:9). Knowing the personal responsibility we have in this process means we need to open the eyes of our hearts so that we "may know what is the hope to which he has called [us]" (Eph. 1:18).

God understands how we think and feel. He relates to us. God is "near to the brokenhearted and saves the crushed in spirit" (Ps. 34:18). God saw and comforted Hagar and didn't ignore her despair. He visited her, empathized with her, and lifted her eyes to the greatest truth in her experience. God understands how we feel, but his character isn't defined or changed by our feelings.

Sometimes our minds and hearts contradict how God views a situation. It is always best to choose God's way even if it doesn't make sense. We can be facing a harrowing crisis or significant trial, and he asks us to be filled with joy (James 1:2–4). We may be facing an uncertain future, but we don't have to fear (Isa. 41:10).

Negative thoughts and emotions can emerge from our experiences, but ultimately, we must pull them in line with God's truth. Saying yes to trusting God, even when we think and feel that there are reasons not to, takes us one step closer to God's best. *Yes* is a simple three-letter word on which the hinge of history swings. It's our choice whether to say yes to God; he won't make us cooperate. But saying yes changes our lives and the lives of those around us.

When Your Yes Collides with Heaven

Her tweet read, "to answer all your questions, yes, Thanksgiving year 7 is planned out." Seven years before, Wanda Dench, intending to communicate with her grandson, accidentally sent Jamal Hinton a text message inviting him to eat Thanksgiving dinner with her. Hinton, skeptical that the text was from his real grandmother, needed confirmation. When Dench sent a photo of herself, Hinton replied with laughter via an emoji and a response saying, "You're not my grandma."

Dench didn't let her accidental text to Hinton get in the way. She said he could still come to dinner if he wanted to. And he did. For several years. And then in 2020, a few months after Dench's husband passed away, Hinton posted a video to YouTube of him and his girlfriend sharing the special day with Wanda. In addition to joining her for Thanksgiving, Jamal went with her when she got her first tattoo at age sixty-five. Their friendship grew, and last I knew, it was seven years in a row that they spent their Thanksgiving holiday together. Jamal said yes to an invitation and found a friend.[3]

On Christmas Eve a few years back, western New York was being pummeled by a severe winter storm. Sha'Kyra Aughtry was home when she heard screams coming from outside. Looking through her window, she saw a man standing in the blinding blizzard conditions, crying out for help.

Aughtry's boyfriend went outside and carried Joe White, a sixty-four-year-old developmentally disabled man, into her home and out of the dangerous cold. Something had happened and Joe became disoriented and confused, placing himself right in the middle of a life-threatening storm. His hands were blistered and in pain.

She used her hair dryer to melt ice off his hands. She called for first responders, but no one arrived due to the severity of the storm. No one could get out. It was a dire situation. Joe needed medical attention from trained professionals, and Sha'Kyra didn't know what else to do. She became increasingly worried for his health, so she livestreamed on Facebook and the right people saw it. People came, plowed out the snow, and helped her get Joe to the hospital. Although he suffered from fourth degree frostbite, he recovered. Sha'Kyra said yes to helping a stranger and saved someone's life.[4]

One of the most profound yeses I've ever heard about happened during World War I. On Christmas Eve, opposing forces on the western front were shivering outside in freezing, narrow trenches.

Months of terror due to chemical warfare, hand-to-hand combat, and seemingly endless explosions night after night were the norm. We know details of what happened next from a British soldier named Bruce Bairnsfather. Around 10:00 p.m., the British heard the sound of Christmas caroling coming from the German army. A few British soldiers joined in. A loud voice shouted in English in a thick German accent, "Come over here." A British officer replied with a request to meet halfway.

Slowly and hesitantly, soldiers from both sides risked their lives and crawled out of the trenches to meet in the middle of the battlefield. Typically, anyone crossing no-man's-land was risking life and limb. But on this day, soldiers shook hands and spoke like brothers to one another.

It came to be known as the Christmas Truce. An article in the *Guardian* on Boxing Day 1914 read, "Every acre of meadow under any sort of cover in the rear of the lines was taken possession of for football."[5] Soldiers traded supplies and sang songs. Something similar also occurred between French, German, British, and Belgian soldiers in many other places for hundreds of miles across the western front. Tens of thousands of soldiers said yes to peace that day.

One German soldier verbally accosted and chided his peers for participating in peaceful activities with the enemy. He said, "Such a thing should not happen in wartime. Have you no German sense of honor left?"[6] That German soldier was a young twenty-five-year-old named Adolf Hitler. Unfortunately, history also revealed the power of saying yes to the wrong thing.

It's important to say yes to the right thing.

Things don't just work out in the end because we long for them. But since hope is the anchor of our souls (Heb. 6:19), we are required to tenaciously pursue what God says is accessible. Walter Brueggemann, a scholar on the Old Testament, described hope as trust in both what God did and what he will do, in spite of contrary evidence.[7]

Let God open the eyes of your heart and show you the evidence, not only of what is next but also of what is possible. Then courageously say yes to God's invitation, looking for what he has in store for you next. Like that farmer in the Sahel, dare to believe the harvest will come and endure until it does.

6

THE MIRACLE OF ENDURANCE

Faith takes the first step. Enduring hope helps faith take the second and third.

Often, my travels take me to unusual places and unpredictable circumstances. Once while sitting in a vehicle in a developing nation, a riot broke out and turned the road into a war zone. I was afraid.

During a different trip in another country, tanks and soldiers lined the streets because the government changed its constitution.

Visiting refugee camps filled with hundreds of thousands of people fleeing traumatic scenarios is so overwhelming that I'll never forget these experiences.

On one particular trip to Europe, however, as we drove up to the gate, I was more nervous than I'd been in a long while. On a picture-perfect day and surrounded by beautiful architecture, I was about to step into a meeting with a global political leader and wasn't sure what to expect.

It took months to prepare for this moment. I prayed, asking God for wisdom while preparing for various scenarios. It is a bit ironic when you think of it—being nervous to meet with another human while the God of the universe resides within you.

Guards in full body armor flanked the gate. Their faces were stoic, and their machine guns were perfectly tilted as their helmets reflected the sun. One soldier approached with a pen and clipboard and leaned into our automobile, while another soldier extended a long mirror underneath our car to look for bombs. The bomb-sniffing dog followed. We gave our names and opened our passports, and the guard checked our names against the list.

Getting your name on that list isn't easy. You can't just show up and ask for a conversation. We were welcomed because of the recommendation of two diplomats. The months leading up to the visit were filled with background checks, security reports, confirmation after confirmation, and I'm sure a host of other things I will never know about. It was a relief when our names were found on the list. It meant I hadn't flown halfway around the world, through the night, for nothing. We were about to have an audience with an earthly king.

Once cleared, we walked into the building and found another security checkpoint—metal detector, full-body scan, more dogs who walked around and sniffed, more soldiers with machine guns, and another clipboard. As we walked into an ornately decorated room, one of the leaders greeted us. The paintings on the walls obviously hadn't come from a box store down the road. The fireplace was stoked, the Persian rug enormous, and the chandelier massive. I almost pulled up a chair but noticed our host remained standing. So I followed suit. We stood there—for a while.

After some hidden signal, the leader walked into another room where we sat down at a large table to converse. There were four of us in the room—three listened to the one who had the authority and power to impact a lot of lives. I took notes for further planning, and about halfway through our discussion, I noticed a fifth guest in the room. A spider was crawling up a web that was affixed to the chandelier. I think I was the only one who noticed.

At the end of our discussion, we shook hands and left. When we got outside, I realized that the spider made it into the same meeting I did without all the background checks.

Then I remembered Proverbs 30:28, which says, "The spider skillfully grasps with its hands, and it is in kings' palaces" (NKJV). The spider didn't get the prized internship nor does it have a PhD. It has no relational network. Yet, it was in the company of a sought-after world leader. How?

Two things come to mind. First, it functioned and lived according to its design. I am too heavy to climb on a web, but the spider can do it without any problem. Everything and everyone has a unique design. This includes you. Significance and meaning are found when we live according to our design, regardless of how broken we think we are. God created us to be whole. The broken areas in our lives are not his fault. Yet those very broken places put his love on display just like broken pieces of glass fitted into a work of stained glass art become beautiful when light shines through them. The gifts you have, strengths you exhibit, and even your divinely placed weaknesses are all a result of God's handiwork. For these reasons, we don't hide things that used to be broken. They are part of the story God is telling.

The second reason the spider was able to live where most are unable to visit is because regardless of how long it took or how much effort was needed, the spider endured. There it was—slowly moving through the air, weaving its web, just as it was created to. Eventually, the spider completed its web, then disappeared. It was able to finish because it endured in the work it was given to do.

You are designed to place all of your hope in God. When you do, regardless of what you face, you will inherit the promise in Romans 15:4: "Through endurance and through the encouragement of the Scriptures we might have hope." By looking at God's character in Scripture, we learned that we have hope because of who God is. This verse reveals that without endurance our hope will be incomplete.

Hebrews 6:11–12 says, "And we desire each one of you to show the same earnestness to have the full assurance of hope *until the end*, so that you may not be sluggish, but imitators of those who through faith and patience inherit the promises" (emphasis added). Abraham obtained God's promise for his life because he was willing to endure (v. 15).

God Designed You

God designed you to hope and to endure. Nehemiah had God-given strengths and was granted permission by his earthly king to rebuild the wall. But Nehemiah also possessed God-given weaknesses. Both his strengths and weaknesses played a role. God chose him not only for things he was good at but also for things he wasn't. Nehemiah didn't pretend to be an architect and sketch blueprints for the new wall. He was a cupbearer to the king. Nehemiah understood that God doesn't bless pretense. So he simply walked among the rubble. As he went, he saw something different, something God could build with, and he began working. There were plenty of opportunities to become discouraged and distracted and to lose hope. But it's hard to lose faith and hope when it lives within you. Nehemiah's life is what endurance looks like.

Dick Foth, an author, speaker, and friend, tells a well-known story of what endurance looks like. In the 1960s, there was a race to be the first nation to put someone on the moon. President John F. Kennedy mobilized our country behind this cause. On a trip to Florida where he planned to check on the progress of the lunar mission, the president met a janitor sweeping the floor. When he asked the man what his job was, he responded, "I'm helping to put someone on the moon."

What did the janitor recognize that many of us overlook? Pulling all-nighters to calculate equations and faithfully sweeping floors with little notoriety both require a vital ingredient if you're going to put someone on the moon: endurance.

Endurance requires admitting our weaknesses. The apostle Paul doesn't boast about his strengths but rather his weaknesses: "For the sake of Christ, then, I am content with weaknesses, insults, hardships, persecutions, and calamities. For when I am weak, then I am strong" (2 Cor. 12:10). Why does Paul feel strong when he is weak? In verse 9 he says God's power is "made perfect in weakness."

Paul isn't settling for dysfunction in his life. He isn't using the existence of weakness as an excuse to adopt a new normal and become spiritually lazy. He understands that when we function according to our design, we find power beyond what natural ability can achieve. But acknowledging weakness isn't just about accepting the way God designed us. It's also about what he accomplishes through our unique design.

Stained glass windows are mesmerizing to look at. They are intricate, delicate, artistic, and originally practical. Centuries ago, only clergy had access to the Scriptures. Stained glass wasn't only decorative and exquisite. It told biblical stories in a visual way for the illiterate. Once illuminated, God's character was revealed through colorful, artistic symbols.

Before the invention of electricity, sunlight was functional and also a symbol of heaven and the divine good. It was reminiscent of the first thing God created in Genesis 1 as light separated the darkness. For these primary reasons, by the eleventh century, stained glass was the most widespread and popular art form in Europe. The windows reinforced weekly church teaching.

The detailed craftsmanship of this lost art form is priceless. We all pause and stare whenever we see it. Broken pieces of glass, all uniquely colored and shaped, are put together to creatively tell the story of God in a language all can understand. The art is meticulously crafted for one reason: for light to shine through it. Without the light, the glass is useless.

Just as Nehemiah used the bits of glass and the jagged stones from the rubble to rebuild the wall, our heavenly Father assembles the shards from your past into something special. Your design may not seem impressive to you, but God put you together for a reason and a purpose. When God's light shines through you, your hardships and broken places become beautiful. Your vulnerable hope in God makes you a stained glass soul. God shines through you.

God Has Hope Too

Joshua Bell, an acclaimed musician, performs in some of the world's most prestigious halls and theatres where people pay a premium to hear him play. But what if he played on an ordinary day surrounded by routine activity?

Well, when given the opportunity to hear him one day in 2007, 1,070 people walked by him and paid no attention. He stood in a DC subway playing a $3.5 million violin and only 27 people stopped.[1] One of them was a three-year-old child. Of all who walked right by him, hearing him play, only one person recognized him. The story caught the attention of millions and reminded us all to slow down and notice the beauty around us. Seven years after the experiment, Mr. Bell tried it again.

This time, things were different. He wasn't disguised in casual clothing and a baseball cap. It wasn't a social experiment. Rather, it was a way to advocate for music education. The media knew beforehand and publicized the time and date he would play. Accompanied by nine students from the National YoungArts Foundation, Bell played a thirty-minute session. People gathered around, some recognizing the Grammy-winning artist, and the crowd noticed the beauty they heard.[2]

Mr. Bell learned a lot from his initial experience in 2007. Before that, he would walk past street musicians, unaware of their true experience. Now Bell says, "I'm sometimes occasionally recognized by the street performers, and they say 'hey, thanks for that experiment because [since then] people are a little bit more aware of what we're doing here.'"[3] Not only do the other musicians often recognize him, but he now "sees" them too.

Likely, I would have walked right past Joshua Bell not only the first time but the second time too. While I like music, I couldn't tell the difference between a fifty-dollar violin or one a world-renowned musician plays on.

But God is different than I am. He never walks past anyone. To God, no one is ordinary. He sees with impeccable accuracy how crucial you are to your family, community, and the stranger you may meet today. Your intrinsic, significant value is immeasurable, and it has nothing to do with how well you perform or who notices you. Your value has to do with what lies within you. Christ in you is eternal and immeasurable. Colossians 1:27 says Christ in you is the "hope of glory." Did you catch that? The glory of God has *hope* and it involves *Christ in you.*

The construction worker, professor, and junior high student; the dad running an errand; the businesswoman taking her company public; and everyone else have the opportunity to see the story of God unfold. When you ignore, overlook, or disbelieve that God chose you, someone will miss the unique expression of Christ in you, the hope of glory. God wants to work deeply within you to impact the hopelessness in the lives of those around you. The hope of the world lives inside you and asks you to open up and let the world see it. What does it look like for your stained glass soul to shine?

Now is the time to let go of all insecurity, feelings of insignificance, self-doubt, and shame and to move forward in your inheritance. Make the decision to place all your hope in God and say yes, through faith, to once again pursue God's promises.

Go find some rubble or pieces of glass and create something with God. What qualifies you has nothing to do with you; it has to do with who designed you. Jeremiah puts it this way: "Let not the wise man boast in his wisdom, let not the mighty man boast in his might, let not the rich man boast in his riches, but let him who boasts boast in this, that he understands and knows me, that I am the LORD who practices steadfast love, justice, and righteousness in the earth. For in these things I delight, declares the LORD" (Jer. 9:23–24). You were designed to be the catalyst of a collision between heaven and humanity.

Follow Jesus's Example

Much of what we know about Jesus comes from the book of Isaiah in the Old Testament. In chapter 6, after Isaiah volunteers again to continue his work, God opens the eyes of his heart in profound ways.

Jesus quotes Isaiah 61:1 when he says, "The Spirit of the Lord is upon me, because he has anointed me" (Luke 4:18). Why did God anoint Jesus? Keep reading Luke, and you will see that Jesus's anointing involves bringing hope to others. While alive, Jesus walked on water, healed people's diseases, and raised the dead. He stood up against injustice and gender inequality. He loved and served the marginalized. He met human need with immeasurable love. He is our example of what we should do. Through us, he still does these things when our stained glass souls shine: Christ in us—the hope of glory.

If there ever was a man who walked the face of the earth whose life and integrity are worth emulating, it is Jesus. I am thankful for his mercy and grace, but they are not excuses to live however we please. Rather, they serve as the primary motivation for you and me to refuse to settle for anything less than heaven on earth. I have a long way to go, but I am committed to continuing on.

The good news is that we don't have to work to bring heaven to earth alone. Although Jesus lived a perfect life and set the example for us to follow, he did not do so merely in his own strength. Jesus cooperated with the Spirit of God. Cooperation with the Spirit sounds mystical and only for spiritual elites. It isn't. It is practical, doable, and starts right now. Even before we learn who God designed us to be, working with God is built into our design.

For example, Luke 5:16 tells us Jesus often went away alone to spend time with God in prayer. This is something you and I can do. We can talk to God anytime, anywhere. Jesus created a rhythm in his life to make prayer a priority. Prayerlessness is a saboteur in so many Christians' lives. We brush our teeth regularly because we know it prevents tooth decay and eliminates bad breath. We hydrate after exercise because it is essential to recovery. When it comes to praying, though, many seem to struggle. Why?

Some of us simply don't know how important it is to partner with God in prayer. The purpose of prayer isn't just about receiving an answer. It has much more to do with humbling ourselves and acknowledging our dependence on God and our desire to know him intimately. Some things happen whether we pray or not. The sun rose this morning, and I didn't ask God to do it. You didn't either. But some things will not happen unless we pray. So pray as if everything hinges on prayer.

When we take a step of faith, sometimes we assume we will end up where God wants us to be simply because we took one step. It doesn't always work that way. Jesus didn't pray once. He did so regularly because he understood we must abide in the vine in order to bear lasting fruit (John 15:5). Prayer isn't begging God for answers. It isn't striving for approval. It is one way we function according to our design. We were created to know him by confidently asking, seeking, and knocking (Matt. 7:7–12). We ask, knowing God is our ultimate provider. We seek because God knows the answers. When we knock, doors open to rooms we didn't know existed.

Prayer keeps our frailty in front of us, and when we are anchored in hope, prayer creates appropriate dependence on God. We can step out in faith to pray because God anointed us. But the beautiful thing is that every time we pray, the Spirit brings additional insight and trust to live out our enduring faith. Cultivating a rhythm of prayer in our lives is vital if we want the light to shine through our broken pieces.

Consistent prayer is one of many examples of what being anointed by God produces. Another is telling the truth regardless of how uncomfortable it may be. We can look to how Jesus lived for other examples. He didn't change his opinion based on who was in the room. He walked in love even when his friends betrayed him. His life reveals how remarkably practical God's anointing can be. I like to put it this way: The more spiritual we are, the more practical we become.

When Heaven and Earth Collide

So what is the anointing?

Simply put, the anointing is when the resources of heaven, deposited within us, flow through us. Anointing oil is used when praying for the sick throughout Christian tradition. Typically, someone puts a small amount of oil on the tip of a finger, touches the forehead, and prays. It is more than a symbol when it becomes a point of faith. The concept of the anointing goes further than this, however. Biblically speaking, anointing means to smear something with oil to set it apart for God's purpose. Imagine being doused with a few gallons of olive oil before walking into work or school one day.

What would happen? It would certainly change your appearance, likely flatten your hair, and definitely stain your clothes. It would also cause you to leave a trail. Everyone would know where you've been based on the trail you leave. That's the point of God's anointing. In your life, you leave a trail, and it creates curiosity in those around you. They begin to wonder why your marriage, once falling apart, is now thriving. They are curious how you overcame your addiction or left behind your anxiety. When they follow the trail of your life, they don't end up at your doorstep; they arrive at God's. His power is perfected, or literally "made complete, finished"[4] in our weakness.

We can easily develop functional dysfunction, which is when we adopt a new normal to justify our lack of evidence for what God promised us. The life Jesus lived should be the pattern for our new normal. We need the Spirit of God to help us in our parenting, in our marriages, with our finances, in our choices, and in every single area of our lives. The anointing can bring deep healing to trauma and provide creativity to the artist. Cures for diseases, business solutions, even new ideas to transform communities come when we partner with God.

Can we function and excel without the anointing? Yes, we can. We can even be successful according to the world's standards. But we will only be successful at what matters to God and in all of eternity when we stop trying on our own. The anointing of the Holy Spirit is not a luxury; it is a necessity.

In my book *The Sacred Chase*, I describe how we enter the kingdom of God and God's best through a door. Jesus is the doorway to salvation. Once we walk through that door, we discover how vast and never-ending is all that God wants to do in and through us. How far we walk, how deep we go, and how surrendered we are is up to us. We are as close to Jesus as we want to be.

You were designed to be anointed by the Spirit of God to demonstrate to those around you what happens when the resources of heaven fuel someone's life. The anointing isn't mystical or spooky. It is when the ordinary is infused with the reality of God. If Jesus needed to be equipped with and empowered by the Spirit of God, how much more do we?

Enduring Hope

The apostle Paul understood how important the anointing of God was. In the first century, in what is now the western coast of Turkey, the city of Ephesus was thriving. It was the most prosperous region of the Roman Empire. Traders and travelers alike found fortune there partially because of the extensive road system, river, and harbor. It was home to the famed Temple of Artemis and Olympic-style games.

The culture was also very spiritual. Astrology, superstition, and a unique blend of black arts filled the city with priests, magicians, and god-seekers from every creed and belief. It is from Ephesus that Paul writes to friends in the city of Corinth, "For the weapons of our warfare are not of the flesh" (2 Cor. 10:4). And to Ephesus from Rome, he writes, "For we do not wrestle against flesh and blood, but against . . . spiritual forces of evil in the heavenly places" (Eph. 6:12). In a modern city, Paul acknowledges the reality of what is unseen.

As was his custom, Paul went to the synagogue in Ephesus to share the life and message of Jesus (Acts 19:8–12). It didn't go very well. Some rejected him and he departed. I'm reminded of this saying: "The same sun that hardens the clay melts the wax." In other words, the condition of our hearts largely predetermines how we will respond to the truth of God. Paul leaves the synagogue and does something unusual. He makes his way to a place called the Hall of Tyrannus.

This was a social gathering place, modeled from the Socratic method, where intellectual, political, and philosophical lectures were given in the afternoons. Paul was one of the teachers, and he would have shared the truths of the gospel we read about in his New Testament writings. The transformation in lives was so profound, so significant, that verse 10 says, "All the residents of Asia heard the word of the Lord, both Jews and Greeks." The Roman province of Asia, an area larger than California, was impacted by one anointed man who did what he was made to do. During this season, somehow, someway, churches in places like Laodicea were started, likely by unnamed Christians who wandered into the Hall of Tyrannus along the way and heard Paul's teaching. The unusual part isn't what was accomplished—but how.

By trade, Paul was a tentmaker, gaining skills as an adolescent apprentice like other young Jewish men. Upon the completion of training, he would have received the appropriate tools needed for his vocation. We know from history that Paul continued his studies, now not as a tentmaker but under a renowned rabbi named Gamaliel. Paul became a member of the Pharisaic sect. With an elite education and career path, Paul was on his way to national prominence.

Then Jesus redefined what success looked like for Paul. The story of Paul's conversion is recorded in Acts 9. He begins to follow Jesus fully, and it isn't always easy. He loses his stable source of income as a Pharisee and experiences marginalization from almost every direction. Those who used to be his closest friends abandon him. Even other Christians are adversarial. By the time Paul comes to Ephesus, things are not going very well for him. What does he do? He doesn't quit. He endures.

Extraordinary Miracles

Paul worked tirelessly as a tentmaker. He tied the handkerchief to his head, day after day, to keep the sweat from the hard labor away from his eyes. The apron, composed of thick leather, held his tools and protected him from bludgeoning with a knife or awl. The handkerchief and apron were associated with the labor, toil, and struggle Paul endured as he lived his life with God. Being a tentmaker wasn't his long-term plan, yet there he was, day after day, faithfully saying yes to God in the way he knew how to. Then the miracles began. Acts 19 says God worked "extraordinary miracles through Paul" (v. 11). What did God use? It wasn't a priestly robe, prayer shawl, speaking ability, or highly prized education. God used dirty, stained work clothes.

The handkerchief and apron represent Paul's determination not to listen to the wrong voice. As a former Pharisee, Paul was taught he shouldn't engage in manual labor or speak about God publicly in marketplaces. But what did Paul do? He became a tentmaker and shared the gospel in the Hall of Tyrannus. Paul ignored the voice from his past that was inferior to God's best.

What do you need to stop listening to from your past? There is treasure buried within every single disappointment and heartbreak. This treasure is the voice of truth, spoken in love, coming from heaven directly to you.

Paul's tent-making tools also represent endurance. Just imagine it. Day after day, toiling and laboring with very little evidence that his work mattered. Some likely walked past him, jeering and saying, "That's the one I heard speaking in the Hall. Supposedly he encountered Jesus long after Jesus was crucified. He went on and on about how good God is. Well, if God is so good, why can't Paul fit in at the synagogue or get a better paying job? Look at him struggle. There is no way God chose him."

In the face of his broken circumstances, Paul didn't quit. He didn't allow hopelessness to set in. Instead, he allowed faith and hope to agree with each other. He surrendered to an unrelenting God who always draws near to the broken-hearted. Paul was willing to undergo criticism from those around him and to ignore any discouragement from within him in order to follow God, even when it didn't make sense.

Your handkerchief and apron represent being honest with who you are and refusing to pretend to be someone you are not. As with Paul and his handkerchief and apron, God doesn't anoint who you pretend to be or who others perceive you to be. God anoints who he created you to be. There are many times in life where what is needed isn't an epic moment. Rather, the moments that create change are often the ones when we make the subtle choice to be who we are. What Dr. Ramata Sissoko Cisse, a college professor in Georgia, did is a great example of this.[5]

Dr. Cisse, an assistant professor of biology for anatomy and physiology at Georgia Gwinnett College in Lawrenceville was contacted by a concerned student who said she couldn't attend class since she didn't have a babysitter. She asked if she could bring the baby to class with her. Knowing how committed she was as a student, the professor approved. The following morning, as Dr. Cisse watched the mom struggle to hold the baby and take class notes during the three-hour lecture, something special happened, and she acted on an idea. Having grown up in Mali, the professor knew how to securely carry babies on her back. Pausing her lecture, she stepped over to the student, picked up the baby, and wrapped the child onto her own back. The little gentleman slept peacefully. Helping a young mom with her baby isn't in the job description of a professor, but Dr. Cisse is more than a professor. There is much more to the design God has for all of us.

Paul's handkerchief and apron represented his determination and endurance. To the former addict, your freedom from addiction is your handkerchief and apron. To the mom folding laundry, your prayers for your family are your handkerchief and apron. To the single dad who overcame depression, vulnerably reapplying for a job is your handkerchief and apron. For the discouraged pastor who struggles to reconcile the gospel with much that is experienced in the Western church, guarding your heart from cynicism is your handkerchief and apron. To anyone who said goodbye to hopelessness and discouragement, God is already working unusual and extraordinary miracles in your life. We have hope because of who God is and what God does with what we give him. When we endure, our hope is made complete.

7

LISTEN CAREFULLY TO
THE INTERRUPTION

Often when we're in the middle of difficult situations, we long for some sort of explanation, direction, or glimmer of hope from God. As we've already discussed, the first step isn't up to God usually; it is up to us. Like Moses, we must "turn aside" because that is when God speaks. Like Moses, our next step is to spiritually hear. In Exodus 3:4, God spoke to Moses only after he turned aside at the burning bush.

God often withholds his voice until we lean in and see beyond our situation. When hopelessness tries to paralyze us, it often says things like, "If God would just tell me what to do, things would turn out better." So we wait to hear God's voice while God is waiting for us to first turn aside.

Your world is full of divine interruptions. With the eyes of your heart wide open, look closely. As you do, God has something to say. As you listen carefully, there are three heart postures you want to have. First, surrender your life to God.

Say yes to God no matter what it costs. Second, trust God. Believe God when he speaks, taking him at his word, believing him beyond your current experience. Third, maintain intimacy with God.

The Right Bus

I met Ahmed at a refugee center where people from Afghanistan, Iraq, Syria, Turkey, and Yemen found their way to escape war, flee radicalism, and attempt to start a new life for themselves and their families. When his shift ended and he finished serving meals to the hundreds of people in line, Ahmed sat down for some tea with me and a few others, and I listened to their stories.

Ahmed sat, smiling, with a heart full of love for those around him. A few months away from his wedding, he anticipated starting a family soon after. He overflowed with the gratitude that accompanies surrender. He was grateful to be seen by God and to know God personally. You would never know where he came from, nor would you believe it if you were told unless it was all verified. I verified it. His story is true.

Now war-torn and devastated by terrorism, Ahmed's country of origin still held fond memories from his childhood. He remembered eating falafel out of a paper bag as a child and the sweetness of mint tea among friends. As a former Olympian, he served his country with pride in the games. As a former mentor in the Special Olympics, he saw potential inside everyone.

When radicalism took the lives of tens of thousands across the Middle East, his nation was front and center during the evening news. It often still is. Known by his government as an elite athlete, Ahmed was conscripted to serve in the special forces to defend his land. During his combat tour, the atrocities he observed and sought to prevent became too much. He couldn't unsee what had been done to women and children. After finishing military service, he sought to leave his country to try to escape his memories.

For months, he took buses, hitchhiked, and worked odd jobs to save enough money for the next phase of his journey. He had in mind a particular European country where he hoped to start a new life. He didn't have anything left back home. But he knew of only two options to get to his final destination: either find a way to travel by boat or cross through enemy-occupied lines, one checkpoint after the other, then pay someone to smuggle him into Europe. He chose the second option as it seemed the most attainable.

For weeks, Ahmed journeyed across enemy-occupied territory. At each checkpoint, whether he traveled by vehicle, foot, or animal, he was forced to show paperwork. On one day, a voice inside his heart prompted him to take a particular bus. The bus stopped at a checkpoint that was different. Ahmed looked out and saw multiple soldiers with weapons in hand separating passengers from the vehicles in front of them. Some passengers were allowed to get back on while others were either executed or taken away. Ahmed was convinced his life would soon end, and he wondered what voice had told him to get on this particular bus.

He knew the soldiers were checking names against a database. The passengers on his bus exited, stood in line, and waited. When the time came for Ahmed to present his papers, an elderly woman stepped off the bus and began to yell at the soldiers. Rather than arrest or harm her, they respected her. She demanded they leave Ahmed alone. For some reason they did. Ahmed climbed back onto the bus, sat at the front, and they drove on.

He was given his life back. When they reached the end of the road, he waited outside of the bus door to thank her. She never got off the bus. Ahmed climbed back on, looking up and down each row and in each seat, but he didn't see her. He asked the driver where she went or if she had exited through the back door. The driver informed him no passenger on his bus fit Ahmed's description.

Fifteen months later, after working odd jobs, he paid fifteen hundred euros for a boat ride to Europe. Homeless and awaiting opportunity to become a legal refugee, he stood in line at one of Convoy of Hope's feeding programs. He heard one of the volunteers quote the words of Jesus: "Love your enemies" (Matt. 5:44). In that moment, he thought, *Jesus must be God for only God would ask me to do something impossible like love my enemies.* That evening, Ahmed heard the gospel and placed his hope in God.

As Ahmed recounted what happened to him that night, he told me he believed the elderly woman who had gotten off the bus was an angel sent by God to protect him. He also said the voice that had told him to take that particular bus on that day was the same voice that spoke to his heart when he heard the gospel. Last I knew, he still serves other refugees, telling them about God and his friend from the bus. Ahmed is a great example of how sometimes we say yes to God even before we understand.

Surrender

Obedience says yes to God after he speaks. Surrender says yes to God beforehand. Surrender is a heart posture. God has a habit of interrupting humanity when hope is hard to find, and we are given two choices: surrender to God or succumb to hopelessness. He interrupted Adam and Eve in the garden when they hid in shame. He interrupted Moses at the burning bush after forty years of being haunted by failure. And he interrupted Philip at the height of his success.

Approximately five years after the death and resurrection of Jesus, "there arose on that day a great persecution against the church in Jerusalem, and they were all scattered throughout the regions" (Acts 8:1–2). Philip, a servant leader in the early church, went to Samaria where he shared the gospel. Remarkable miracles took place. Of all places where something like this might occur, Samaria wouldn't have been on anyone's radar. The first-century Jewish and Samaritan communities were deep enemies. But Philip watched God transform people so that "there was much joy in that city" (v. 8).

Philip was at the apex of success, you could say, when an angel told him to leave the city and go south to a road leading to Gaza (v. 26). The direction would put Philip in the middle of the desert. Alone. Isolated. Far away from what God was demonstrably doing in Samaria. In Samaria, Philip saw the fruit of his labor. He worked hard and it paid off. Then God asked him to walk away, give it all up, and go elsewhere.

Are you willing to surrender and lay everything down if heaven interrupts you? What might it look like for you to slide the script you've written for your life to the side because of a divine interruption?

I count eighteen occurrences in the book of Acts when God provides extraordinary leading, which requires extraordinary surrender from his people. This is one of those instances. Philip leaves it all and travels to the desert alone, heading toward Gaza as he was told.

But Philip never arrived where he was headed. Instead, he was supernaturally directed by the Spirit of God to Azotus, which is twenty miles north of Gaza. How strange is that?

God told him to go somewhere, and then God completely diverted him from there. But we don't see Philip acting concerned or frustrated in any way. Why? Because of what took place between Azotus and Gaza. Philip experienced another divine interruption.

This time, it wasn't an angel who spoke to him in the desert. It was the Spirit of God telling Philip to go near a chariot he saw in the distance (v. 29).

An Ethiopian man was returning home after a pilgrimage to Jerusalem. We don't know his name; however, Acts 8 describes him as serving in the court of the queen. This man was reading the scroll of the prophet Isaiah and did not fully understand what he was reading. Only those of extreme wealth or prominence had access to scrolls like this one. He had just visited the church in its early stage and had left still not knowing who Jesus truly was. To read Isaiah meant the Ethiopian knew Hebrew. This royal official was not a random visitor. He had history and knowledge about God but didn't know who Jesus was.

The Spirit of God saw the Ethiopian leaving Jerusalem and saw Philip somewhere between Samaria and Gaza. God sees us all. He knew beforehand he could count on Philip to say yes. Philip surrendered, listened, obeyed, and drew near to the chariot.

From the writings of Isaiah that the Ethiopian was reading, Philip shared who Jesus was (v. 35) and baptized him. Church historian Irenaeus tells us the Ethiopian was the first to share the gospel in his country.

Significance is found in surrender.

Philip did not end up in Gaza, the destination he had set his face toward, because he lived a yielded life. We never see a time when he argues with God. This tells me Philip's yes came long before God said anything.

Regardless of who you are and what your experience is, responding to a divine interruption is not only good but also right. Moving with God may lift you out of your personal hopelessness, as it did for Adam and Eve, or it may invite you to become a catalyst for change, as in the case of Moses. The impact of your surrender may be highly visible, as it was for Philip in Samaria, or less visible, as it was for him in the desert. Either way, surrender is the step to take. Surrender and say yes to God long before he speaks.

Trust

Surrender to God is grounded in trust. Philip didn't just obey God when he went into the desert; he trusted him. Trust is the second heart posture. When we love God, we do what he says (John 14:23), not from a heart of compliance but one of sincere privilege. Jesus didn't give his life on the cross so we could mimic him with spiritual artificial intelligence.

Part of our inheritance is our adoption into God's family. We are not slaves or employees. We are sons and daughters. We trust what God says because we trust the heart and voice of our good Father. His word and character are inseparable (John 1:1, 14).

Jeremiah was a Hebrew reformer and prophet who lived around the sixth century BC. He lived among the refugees and exiles who survived an ancient holocaust. In Jeremiah 29:11, he records what God said when hopelessness was interrupted: "For I know the plans I have for you, declares the LORD, plans for welfare and not for evil, to give you a future and a hope." You may be familiar with the verse. But there is more going on behind the scenes than many of us are aware of.

Around the year 586 BC, a Babylonian king named Nebuchadnezzar dispatched his army to conquer ancient Israel.

Jerusalem, the shining city of Israel, was destroyed. A young man named Daniel was one of many who were abducted and forced into slavery. Israel ceased to be a nation.

At this time in history, the prosperity of a nation was directly tied to its god. For this reason, for all practical purposes, people thought Yahweh, the God of the Hebrews, was also dead. The temple in Jerusalem, which served as the door to forgiveness and access to God, was destroyed. Israel was humiliated, and the religious traditions the Jews grew up with were deemed illegal.

Those who survived were given new names by the Babylonians—a direct and calculated insult to the Jewish understanding of God. Names meant something significant, and people saw them as a symbol of divine purpose. It would seem the days of the Jews, once written in God's book, would now be recorded under another name by a foreign god.

The book of Daniel, although not in chronological order, strikingly opens with something almost unthinkable. At the height of uncertainty, trauma, and tragedy, the first thing Daniel writes about is his trust in God and how much God is involved in human history: "In the third year of the reign of Jehoiakim king of Judah, Nebuchadnezzar king of Babylon came to Jerusalem and besieged it. And the Lord gave Jehoiakim king of Judah into his hand, with some of the vessels of the house of God. And he brought them to the land of Shinar, to the house of his god, and placed the vessels in the treasury of his god" (1:1–2).

Of all things for Daniel to notice and mention first! He doesn't hold God accountable for the loss of his family, nor does he accuse King Nebuchadnezzar of being a tyrant. Daniel first mentions how it was the *Lord* who gave the land, the temple, and the Judean kingdom into the hand of the foreign army. Daniel isn't blaming God, nor is he holding God accountable for the invasion. The Bible is clear: God removed his protective hand and allowed the choices of ancient Israel to play out. Daniel is simply remembering that even though our days are often the result of the choices we make or that others make toward us, none of them catch God off guard. He knows what is coming. God knows what is taking place now. And we are invited to partner with him to affect the outcome.

This is the context of Jeremiah 29:11. In verse 4, Jeremiah says, "Thus says the LORD of hosts, the God of Israel, to all the exiles whom I have sent into exile from Jerusalem to Babylon." God is not speaking to one individual person. He is speaking to a specific people, belonging to a specific nation, with distinct cultural and religious traditions, who are traumatized by war and have lost everything they hold dear.

In verse 10, Jeremiah says, "For thus says the LORD: When seventy years are completed for Babylon, I will visit you, and I will fulfill to you my promise and bring you back to this place." The loss the Jews experienced was a direct result of years of decisions that violated God's heart and God's preferred plan for them. God wasn't at fault. They were. The Babylonian army was. Still, we see how loving God is. He is standing at the door knocking.

He knows exactly how many years his people will be living in foreign land. Some of them won't leave Babylon alive. Yet God does not walk away from them. God speaks to them as a tender Father. They aren't as alone as they thought. God interrupts his people in their darkest hour with hope: "For I know the plans I have for you, declares the LORD, plans for welfare and not for evil, to give you a future and a *hope*" (v. 11, emphasis added).

After telling his people that they will be refugees for seventy years, God shares what he is thinking with them. It involves two things: a future and a hope.

> Then you will call upon me and come and pray to me, and I will hear you. You will seek me and find me, when you seek me with all your heart. I will be found by you, declares the LORD, and I will restore your fortunes and gather you from all the nations and all the places where I have driven you, declares the LORD, and I will bring you back to the place from which I sent you into exile. (vv. 12–14)

In other words, the choices we make or those made by others can get in the way of God's best for us.

Regardless of how each one of us ended up where we are, God is still thinking about us. He hasn't walked away. His preferred future is still there. He sends yet another invitation to call out to him, to pray and to seek him. He will listen. He will be found. He will restore.

But how do you go from something as traumatic and overwhelming as the destruction of your family, nation, heritage, and personal dreams to the better place known as the future? You trust God.

Like a long and winding road, God's artisan plan is specifically designed to take you to a place uniquely cultivated by him. To the person broken by childhood abuse, his plan will tenderly bring trust and healing back to you. For anyone tormented by depression, he is there waiting and ready to listen. To someone who is steeped in shame and can't seem to let go, God's plan for you involves freedom. To the family waiting for a prayer to be answered, God hears you. To the weary soul, God is still your strength. To the anxious heart, God has a peace that reaches beyond what you can ever understand.

To the wandering and fearful soul in need of wisdom and direction, he has already gone before you and will walk with you every step of the way. He will meet you there—wherever that may be. And to the many who have already experienced what can happen when hope breaks through, others are waiting for you to become part of the answer God has for them.

In Jeremiah 29:11, the word *plan* can also mean *thoughts* (KJV). So the plan is less about God sketching out your life like a blueprint and tucking it away to become a report card. Of course, we are accountable to God for how we live, but that isn't the point of verse 11. It is more about the awesome and humbling truth that the God of the universe knows you.

God is literally thinking about you. Part of his plan involves what your life will look like in twenty years. But his plan isn't just future forward. God's plan is here and now. This is why the Bible says God is "a very present help in trouble" (Ps. 46:1). His plan has everything to do with thinking about you. At this very moment, you're on God's heart and mind.

This is why hope is so powerful. It acknowledges that in real time, this very moment, you can turn your affection toward God in humble vulnerability, and he will not ignore you. His thoughts are much more beautiful, breathtaking, and unimaginable than you can fathom (Eph. 3:20). Like Jeremiah, will you dare to believe God has a future and a hope for you? Will you trust that because God is near, there is always a better day coming? Will you find your hope to endure because God has a preferred future in mind? Can you trust what God says even when your situation seems to convince you not to?

Intimacy

The third heart posture that will help you listen carefully to the right voice is intimacy.

135

When you surrender to God, you "yield to the power . . . of another."[1] When you trust in God, you believe he is "good and honest and will not harm you" and that he is "safe and reliable."[2] Believing God means that what he says, you "consider to be true."[3]

Surrender has everything to do with you and your yieldedness to God. Trust has everything to do with your response to who God is. Intimacy, growing in your face-to-face relationship with God—where you know his heart, hear his voice, believe what he says, and abide in him—is the fruit of your surrender and trust.

One of the greatest enemies of hope is our inability to hear God's voice when things are difficult. We can believe God speaks but miss his voice due to a lack of ongoing intimacy with him.

Abraham is a great example of how we must both intimately listen and wholeheartedly believe. Romans 4:18 says, "Against all hope, Abraham in hope believed and so became the father of many nations" (NIV). The Passion Translation puts it this way: "Against all odds, when it looked hopeless, Abraham believed the promise and expected God to fulfill it." Even when there seems to be no hope, you can allow God to become the epicenter of all you believe to be true. By doing this, hope—in the form of a ram (Gen. 22:1–13)—emerged out of nowhere in Abraham's life. But hope must grow. It never remains dormant. This is why walking intimately with God is important.

Surrendering to God in what you are uniquely facing this moment may look different than it did yesterday. Our lives depend on what God has to say to us now, present tense (Deut. 8:3), just as much as when he first whispered to our hearts. Like Abraham, our spiritual inheritance is tied not only to believing wholeheartedly but also to intimately and continually listening to God's voice (Eph. 1:13). Remember, salvation is not the finish line; it is only the beginning.

Abraham lived in ancient Iraq. For all practical purposes, he was just like every other worshiper of the mythical Babylonian moon god. But one day, Abraham hears God speak to him (Gen. 12:1–3), and he uproots his family and life in response. At this time in history, Abraham doesn't have access to Scripture the way we do. The Ten Commandments haven't been given yet. Moses, Isaiah, Jeremiah, and Esther are in the distant future. Yet Abraham believes a God he barely knows when he speaks.

In Genesis 15, God comes to Abraham again and makes a covenant with him, promising the childless Abraham and his wife, Sarah, a family. Abraham, though well past the childbearing years, "believed the LORD" (v. 6).

Eventually, God miraculously fulfills his promise, and Abraham and Sarah have a son named Isaac. In Genesis 22, God invites Abraham to take Isaac to the land of Moriah and sacrifice him. What would you do if your long-awaited promise was hand-delivered by God and then you were asked to destroy it? Initially, it seems absurd that Abraham did not argue with God. But child sacrifice was common in the land during that time in history. To Abraham, he was being asked to do something supported by many other ancient religious systems. As he will soon see, however, God is not like the other mythical gods.

Quick and eager to please God, Abraham "rose early in the morning" and even cut the wood to be used for the burnt offering which, by the way, was to be his son (vv. 2–3). Scholars don't agree on how old Isaac was at the time. But he was old enough to communicate understandably with his dad (v. 7) as they walked for three days to the mountain. In verse 5, we see evidence that Abraham had hope. He told the other young men with him that both he and Isaac would return to them. Now, wait just a minute.

God told Abraham to take Isaac to a mountain and sacrifice him. Abraham had every intention of doing so. Later in the story, we see evidence that Abraham had no idea what God was about to do. But something on the inside of him was so real, so tangible, that even though he was going to sacrifice his son, he emphatically declared that both he and Isaac would come back (v. 5). Whether he trusted that God would provide another sacrifice or that God could raise his son from the dead, we do not know. What we do know is Abraham demonstrated his hope with faith when he said to his son, "God will provide for himself a lamb" (v. 8).

Abraham climbed the mountain with God's promise at his side. No doubt he endured and fought through any doubts. He even invested the time to complete a small construction project and built an altar. He then kindled a fire. After binding his son and laying him on the altar, he took the knife in his hand, raised it, and was about to do the unthinkable. He was going to take the life of his son and, in so doing, let go of God's promise for him and Sarah after years of watching him grow.

With knife raised and fire kindled, in the time it takes someone to take one breath, God interrupted Abraham.

The angel of the LORD called to him from heaven and said, "Abraham, Abraham!" And he said, "Here I am." He said, "Do not lay your hand on the boy or do anything to him, for now I know that you fear God, seeing you have not withheld your son, your only son, from me."
And Abraham lifted up his eyes and looked, and behold, behind him was a ram, caught in a thicket by his horns. And Abraham went and took the ram and offered it up as a burnt offering instead of his son. (Gen. 12:11–13)

The scene from this remarkable moment is indicative of what God the Father would do when he gave his one and only son as a sacrifice for us (John 3:16–17). The cross is our greatest proof that every promise made by God is kept by God.

Against all hope, Abraham still had hope. He demonstrated his hope with faith that endured. One piece of wood, one step up the mountain, one day after the next on their journey to the place where he would pass the test of spiritual surrender. Abraham did something else, though, something crucial we all must do if hope is going to lead us into our full spiritual inheritance. He listened carefully every time God spoke.

Ears That Hear

Sometimes what God said in the past gets in the way of what God is saying now.

Don't misunderstand. It is important to know what God said and did in the past, and Scripture records what he said and did throughout the ages. What God said is our standard for how we filter his voice from others' voices. God will never say something today that violates the truth of his character as presented in his Word. Scripture, though, is not merely a piece of literature we read intellectually or academically. It is an active (Heb. 4:12), present-tense voice of God in our lives. It is both what God said and what God is saying as we read it with ears tuned in to what the Spirit of truth is teaching us (John 16:13).

The way we stay fully alive in God is not simply by believing what God said but also by believing what God is saying right now. Imagine a husband who only listens to his wife one day and then assumes he knows all there is to know about her, her desires, and her plans. We all know that marriage will shrivel. Similarly, a college football quarter-back who only listens to the coach on the first day of practice and refuses to heed the coach's instructions the rest of the season will likely not perform well. Likewise, hearing God requires daily communication and a growing intimacy with him. We live by every single word that comes from God's mouth (Deut. 8:3). This is why we are told over and over again not to harden our hearts if we hear his voice today (Heb. 3:15). The verse doesn't say to listen to God's voice yesterday. It says today.

God also invites us to have ears to hear what God is saying (Rev. 2:7, 29; 3:22). Scripture assumes both that God speaks and that we are capable of hearing his voice in whatever form it comes. God whispers when we watch a sunset: "Remember, I made that, and I can also make something beautiful from the mess you're in now." God speaks when we hold a newborn baby in our arms: "All the love you feel right now is what I feel, times a billion, when I look at you."

The striking truth of Abraham's story isn't just his bold faith, enduring hope, complete surrender, or childlike trust. The point is he listened when God told him to take his son up the mountain—and he kept listening, intimately, even as he raised his knife in the air. As Abraham walked up the mountain, God saw the other side of the experience. God saw the ram walking up the mountain at just the right time and with just the right speed so that as soon as Abraham heard God speak, the miracle of provision occurred. God always sees both sides of the mountain. Just imagine how differently God's promise to Abraham would have unfolded had Abraham not heard God call out to him when Isaac was on the altar. But, like Philip, Abraham heard God's divine interruption.

We must listen carefully to what God is saying here and now, or we'll miss part of our spiritual inheritance. Like the train of God's robe that keeps filling and filling the temple, there is always another facet of his promise on the way.

You may be at a place where the eyes of your heart are open, and you are clinging to the hope that God isn't finished yet. You choose to have faith that he has only just begun. You look back to find evidence that hope works because of who God is. You too have your Isaac with you, and the future may seem uncertain or even terrifying, but God isn't finished yet. He has something else in store for you.

Keep your ears of faith open. Something is on the other side of your mountain, and God sees it clearly. He will guide you with his voice. Demonstrating bold, childlike faith is tied to hearing his voice of truth above all other voices of preference, assumption, or shame. Your hope in God will take you into your full spiritual inheritance as you surrender your heart, trust God, and maintain intimacy with him.

8

REMEMBER

Surrender, trust, and intimacy are excellent companions to have with us on our journey toward gaining hold of our spiritual inheritance. Expecting divine interruptions is a remarkable way to live and a way of life God honors. But the truth is there are often a few pieces of the rubble we aren't quite sure what to do with. While we can always trust God's heart, sometimes we don't hear his voice and we can't find his face. This is the place called mystery where we allow hope to do its greatest work.

This is going to be a difficult chapter to write. Likely, it will be challenging to read as well. So let's make a deal. I will do my best not to approach a delicate subject with religious jargon, spiritual quips and quotes, or performative triumph. Instead, I will humbly and openly walk with you through something we share in common with every single person—past, present, and future—who walks with Jesus: the evasive answer to the question *Why?*

It is common and convenient today to blame others. We often ask God why, when we should first ask ourselves that question. Sometimes it isn't the fault of others; it may be ours. Sometimes things happen because of the choices we make, and rather than accept responsibility, we spiritualize our actions and ask God why things are less than what he promised. We can also ask God why someone else made that decision that hurt us so deeply. Understanding why still won't ultimately bring peace either. Sometimes we sincerely ask why because we do trust God, we have hope, we don't need to understand why someone else did what they did, but we feel like life would all come together perfectly if we could somehow know the answer.

Why is whispered in the dark, shouted in broad daylight, reflected upon over coffee, and searched for with tears. Why did it happen? Why did she leave? Why did he say that to me? Why did it end that way? Why did my child die when I prayed so hard? Why is the world so broken when we have so many solutions at hand? Why didn't God stop it? I was vulnerable, got my hopes up, and it still fell apart. Why?

Asking why leads to other questions: Where was God when it happened? How could I be so foolish? Will things ever really change? If God is so loving, how could he just sit back and watch?

I once asked God why some of the people I trusted and loved most as a child betrayed me the deepest. I struggle to know why I've overcome so many things in my personal life only to find lingering struggles I must still defeat. Why, after praying since 1995, am I still waiting on God's answer in so many areas of my life?

The first time I visited a refugee camp, I saw a few mothers missing their hands. I asked the women what happened and was told that the rebels in their home country required them to make a choice: their hands or their children. As I listened to them recount their horrific exodus from their war-torn homeland, I also saw some of their children gather around them. The mothers wondered why humanity was so utterly depraved. I do too.

But I've learned I am not the only one who struggles with why. And it isn't just the poor or exiles. I've also sat next to the wealthy and those who supposedly have it all and who feel hopeless and helpless in their personal lives. There is no amount of money or fame they can find that answers their why questions either. Wealth and fame are no match for life's biggest problems. I understand the need to know why, and I also know that in the end, even if the answer comes, it doesn't satisfy.

The good news is God isn't intimidated by our why questions. But there is something much more profound and important than finding the answer to that question. God is often found in that awkward place—a place called mystery.

Mysteries and Tables

In the Greek New Testament, one of the words we can translate into English as "miracle"—in the context of God revealing something in our world that first existed in his—is *mysterion*.[1] This is where our English word *mystery* comes from. When you think of a miracle, what comes to mind? Perhaps someone with a diagnosis of terminal cancer went in for one more test, expecting another dire message, only to see the medical professional stunned by their clear results. Or a shattered relationship found a new beginning through forgiveness and mercy. A surprise financial gift or pay raise came through at the last minute. A couple who wasn't supposed to be able to have children received news that a baby was on the way.

Stories like these are real. God intervenes in ways we don't expect as we partner with him in prayer and lifestyle, watching faith and hope get to work. There are plenty of stories in Scripture of prison doors miraculously opened, raging storms being stilled, supernatural protection from foreign invasion, and the dead being resurrected. God is able to do anything and is still as active in our lives today as he was in ancient times. The miraculous is not just a phenomenon in Scripture. It is our inheritance too. Some miracles come in the life-changing form of us accepting mystery.

Mysterion comes from a derivative meaning "to shut the mouth."[2] In essence, miracles are a space where the hidden purpose of God and our lack of knowing why collide. The experience is real, but we just don't have the words to explain it. God entrusts us with mystery (Matt. 13:11), and the wisdom of God can come in the form of a mystery (1 Cor. 2:7). Some mysteries are hidden and others are revealed (Rom. 16:25–26). The mystery of God's will, which is part of our spiritual inheritance, is now made known because of Jesus (Eph. 1:9). When I think of hope's ability to take us by the hand as we walk through mystery, Psalm 23 comes to mind.

In my book *Grace in the Valley*, I write about the path we walk in life described in Psalm 23. In this psalm, we learn how God acts as our shepherd. Green pastures didn't just exist in ancient Israel when David articulated these words. God, our Good Shepherd, finds these rich places and makes us lie down in them too.

Shepherds lived nomadic lifestyles and did the hard work of scouting out the next pasture where their sheep would live. Shepherds had to see beyond the arid land and imagine what was around the corner. They went before the sheep to remove jagged stones and thorns from the ground to provide space for sleeping and grazing. At times, they even dug canals to irrigate the land. In addition, shepherds watched for and dispatched predators from afar and up close, painstakingly noticing anything that may harm the flock. Like a shepherd, God makes us lie down in green pastures because he knows it is the perfect place for us to be. He was there before us and prepared it just for us. But what do we do when the path, described as "righteous" (v. 3), leads to "the valley of the shadow of death" (v. 4)?

Let's take a look at the order of events. God makes us "lie down in green pastures" (v. 2), and then he walks with us "through the valley" (v. 4). When hopelessness blinds us, it is easy to invert these—walk through green pastures and lie down in the valley. In the valley, when things are hard, we tend to get bogged down asking why. If God is such a good shepherd, why did he lead me here? If God leads me beside still waters, why does it feel like the storm will never stop raging? If God is the one who restores my soul, why do I still feel so broken inside?

When we come into the moments that are hard, full of pain and suffering, laden with uncertainty, when it's difficult to imagine a better day, that's when the perfectly timed truth of Psalm 23 emerges.

Verse 4 says, "Even though I walk through the valley of the shadow of death, I will fear no evil, for you are with me." Hope requires us to live an "even though" and an "I will" life. *Even though* the valley I am walking through is hard and lonely and I struggle to see how my circumstances will ever turn around, my current experience does not change who God is. Hope is part of our spiritual inheritance. It beckons us to say, *I will.* I will what? I will choose to see who is right here with me in this valley—God. He is the one guiding me.

David tells us that it is God himself who prepares a table for us (v. 5). But he doesn't prepare that table—a place full of connection, intimacy, provision, and joy—in the green pasture. No, he prepares the table in the valley. God throws a party for you in your difficult hour as you traverse the valley . . . and he invites your enemy.

I can imagine you walking in the valley. The nights just seem to get longer, and the taunting of your soul's enemies gets louder. Your memories of the green pasture are still there, but you feel as if you've spent so much time in the valley that it has become your permanent home. You even wonder where God is. The valley is full of death's shadow. It is hard to see anything good, let alone find God. You come around the corner and there it is, the table.

Surprised and overwhelmed by his presence, you cry out, "God, what are you doing here?"

He responds, "Oh, my child, I am putting together a celebration and a feast. The final table settings are being arranged."

"But God," you say, "the enemies of my soul are here with us. I often wondered why you felt so close in the green pasture and where you went. I knew you would never leave me. You promised. But I guess I didn't expect to see you here now. I'm sorry, God, that I doubted you."

And then God responds, like he always does when we surrender, trust, and intimately draw near to him: "I invited the enemies of your soul too because they will vanish once you and I sit down at the table together. What seemed like an impossibility was actually an invitation to be with me!"

To be clear, the enemy is ultimately not a person, but it does have a name. Likely, you know the name well. For you, it may be shame or regret or depression or hopelessness. In the valley, surrounded by the enemies who gloat over the difficulties and impossibilities you face, you have a choice. You can allow the need to know why to disillusion you, or you can turn your back on the enemy of your soul, pull up a seat at God's table, and feast. At that point, you may very well find that the valley is suddenly transformed, and the green pasture and the valley are actually the same place.

Spiritual curiosity and a willingness to enter the realm of mystery are often the first ingredients for an adventure with God. When the need to understand emerges from our desire to control the outcome, satisfy our doubt, or shift the blame onto God, it will stifle our ability to find hope and peace. Of course, your questions never threaten God. He is secure in who he is. The train of his robe always fills the temple. Being consumed with the why may not intimidate God, but it can drain your soul. Instead let your why lead you to God.

You aren't alone in your quest to understand. If you're a bit afraid of coming to God with your frustrations, doubts, and concerns, it might be helpful to know others have broken through with the power of hope. Even more helpful is the truth that we don't need to live with doubt ever again.

Job asked God why he was struggling (Job 7:20; 9:29). David asked God why he seemed so far away (Ps. 10:1). Elijah asked why something terrible and heartbreaking happened to a woman (1 Kings 17:20). Even Jesus asked why (Mark 15:34). The circumstances that led you to your why questions are an invitation, hand delivered by heaven, to those who will dare to hope. Proverbs 25:2 says, "It is the glory of God to conceal things [mystery], but the glory of kings to search things out."

Let God pull you closer to his heart where you can learn the mysteries of his ways. His face shines, not only to expose everything in the recesses of your hearts but also to expose the precious diamonds forged during times of pressure and adversity.

Peace Until He Comes

Over the years, whether I'm teaching a group of university students, sharing God's heart for the poor at a church, or speaking at a conference, people want to talk for a few minutes after I'm done speaking. During these moments, I've noticed a pattern. Many think and feel that if they could just understand why, then peace will come. But that isn't true.

Because each one of us sees our world dimly (1 Cor. 13:12), peace doesn't come when we understand. True peace transcends our understanding (Phil. 4:7). How do we lay hold of a peace as rich as that?

First, we have to acknowledge that pain, suffering, and brokenness are pervasive and often a result of the broken world we live in. Jesus said, "Here on earth you will have many trials and sorrows" (John 16:33 NLT).

Jesus is not referring to pain caused to ourselves or others when we ignore wisdom and choose our own way. Jesus never excuses foolishness or wickedness, nor does he ignore the consequences that follow. He told the church in Laodicea why they were lukewarm and clearly articulated to them how he felt about it. Mercy triumphs over judgment, but we also reap what we sow (Gal. 6:7).

The suffering Jesus referred to in John 16 is not due to the hardness of our own hearts per se but is a result of the world we live in. Shakespeare puts it this way: "Each new morn / New widows howl, new orphans cry, new sorrows / Strike heaven on the face."[3] There will be hardships.

Second, to take hold of true peace we must remember that our common human experience is incongruent with God's original intent. Humanity walked with God in the garden. He didn't design us to live with physical, emotional, mental, or spiritual poverty. At the beginning, nothing separated

Adam and Eve from him. There was no sickness, no insecurity, no suffering, and certainly no hopelessness.

Even after hopelessness entered the world through Adam and Eve's choice to turn from God and sever intimate connection with him, all of humanity still reflects God's image, but we do not experience God's original design. Adam and Eve's children were born in their "own likeness" (Gen. 5:3).

The shame that drove them to hide from God can drive all of us into hiding. Yet, as he did with Adam and Eve, God walks toward each one of us as well. This is the good news of the gospel. Because of Jesus, we can forego the ugliness of this life and step into our spiritual inheritance. We can return to the original design.

So, yes, trials and sorrows will come and provide many convincing reasons why we are destined to be spiritually poor, but we don't have to agree. God originally created us for something beautiful. You are a stained glass soul.

Third, we accept our responsibility to partner with God for all things to be restored. This begins when we acknowledge our spiritual condition (Rom. 3:23; 6:23) and, through confession and life change (Rom. 10:9), accept the gift of salvation. This is not the finish line to the Christian life. Salvation is the beginning of a never-ending relationship that starts in this life and continues for eternity. Yes, becoming a new creation in Christ (2 Cor. 5:17) gives us an eternal hope, but we don't have to wait until heaven to start accessing God's original design. To do so is to hold our spiritual inheritance in our hands only to set it on a shelf for decoration. No, we partner with God to pull heaven to earth and believe God's will be done here as it is there (Matt. 6:10).

We pull heaven to earth by holding earth's experience in one hand and heaven's promise in the other. As Jesus said in John 16:33, on the earth we will have trouble. In that

151

same verse, he also says, "But take heart, because I have overcome the world" (NLT). A divine exchange can occur when we stand in between the two truths Jesus mentioned: life's trouble on one side and his overcoming on the other. We pull them together with hope. Nehemiah exchanged rubble for building blocks. Moses exchanged an ordinary walk on an ordinary day beside an ordinary bush for a divine interruption. David exchanged his valley for a banqueting table. When we open the eyes of our heart and see with God's perspective, heaven breaks through into our world, our homes, and our lives.

When we surrender, trust, and live intimately with God, the two realities of here/now and there/then collide. Jesus tells us that in this life we will have trouble, but that isn't the end of the story. If it were, we might naturally ask, "If we are going to have trouble, why even bother getting our hopes up?"

Understanding what Jesus said in John 16:33 requires us to go back and read the beginning of the verse where he says, "I have told you all this so that you may have peace in me" (NLT). Peace. There it is. The peace that transcends understanding.

To be clear, Jesus didn't say he was telling us these things so that we may have peace in our circumstances. He says "that you may have peace in me." In him. We contend prayerfully and hope expectantly for his kingdom to come in our lives. But when we encounter trouble along the way, it no longer defeats us because trouble doesn't surprise us. In John 14:27, Jesus says, "Peace I leave with you; my peace I give to you." We have peace because Jesus already left it here for us.

Peace that surpasses understanding is a peace found in Jesus. It is one of his names—Prince of Peace. To live in the center of a peace like that requires us to let go of, refuse, even forfeit our desire to understand. It means the answer to our why is no longer our quest. Ultimately, I don't need to know why when I know him. When what we know to be true about God doesn't line up with our experience, we dare to hope not only that things can and will change but also that even if they don't, God is still who he says he is.

A Path Paved with Miracles

Sometimes God chooses to never explain why, and that's OK. Some of the greatest miracles in life are not the answers to our prayers or the fulfillment of our hopes. They are those moments when we choose to ignore the voice of hopelessness inside and around us and take our seats at God's table. When God feels absent, we draw near with the assurance that though we may not see his face, we can still see the evidence of his presence.

If you still feel as though you're failing, remember that even the disciples—those who spent almost every day of Jesus's ministry with him—struggled with mystery. At the end of Mark 4, Jesus invites some of his closest friends to get into a boat and cross to the other side. A horrendous storm descends. While Jesus sleeps, the disciples are terrified. Finally, they wake him and ask why he doesn't care that they are about to perish. Then Jesus says to the wind and the sea, "Peace! Be still!" (v. 39).

Notice that he does not say, "Be still, peace." Rather than calming the storm so the disciples can experience peace, he invites peace to come *while* the storm rages. Peace is designed to come and get to work in our lives long before the trials stop, the sorrows fade, and the storms are stilled.

Also notice that Jesus never told the disciples why the storm came or why he slept. What we do know is that Jesus asked them to get into the boat and that he made peace available. Once everyone is settled, Jesus flips the script on them and asks why they were so afraid. Then he spends the next few chapters emphasizing why the disciples never need to be afraid or feel defeated when he's there.

In Mark 5, the disciples watch as a man, severely tormented and bearing the marks of self-mutilation, runs to Jesus. The shame and sheer torment this man lived with didn't prevent him from being vulnerable with God. Sometimes God comes to us and at other times we must run to him. Jesus was not repulsed or embarrassed to be seen in public with this man who was likely naked and covered in blood and scars. Even though the man was probably screaming as he ran toward Jesus, Jesus didn't take a posture of self-defense. He didn't turn and run away. Jesus looked at this broken man and asked for his name. Jesus refused to let the man's issues become the man's identity. The disciples saw Jesus transform someone mentally, emotionally, physically, and spiritually.

Then came a woman who was suffering from a blood disease/disorder. Having spent all her money to get well, she was now poor and living in a hopeless state. Because her sickness made her ceremonially unclean, no one could touch her. When she walked down the street, she would have to shout "Unclean, unclean!" She was vulnerable, suffering, and although in the middle of a large crowd, completely isolated and alone. And then the story in Mark 5 tells us she heard something about Jesus, and it caused her to take a risk. I wonder what she heard about him? If you hear anything about Jesus that intimidates you or prevents you from drawing closer to God, then what you heard isn't true. He is still approachable.

Ignoring the rules, the woman pressed through the crowd to touch him, and upon doing so she was miraculously, mysteriously healed. But Jesus didn't let her sneak off. He made eye contact and called her by name, not the one given to her on earth, but what she was known by in heaven—"daughter" (v. 34).

Then Jesus raises a young girl from the dead (vv. 41–42), feeds a multitude with five loaves of barley bread (the bread of the poor) and two small fish (6:30–44), and defies the law of gravity by walking on water (vv. 45–52).

By Mark 6:56, whether Jesus and his disciples walked in the villages, cities, or rural areas, many people were healed wherever they went. Jesus healed another young girl in Mark 7:29–30 and a deaf man in verses 32–35. In Mark 8, Jesus feeds another multitude in a similar way as before. His compassion on the crowd is undeniable, and his willingness to step into their difficulty is unmistakable. The disciples walked a path paved with miracle after miracle, mystery after mystery.

They walked closely with Jesus for about three years. God's love for those around them was evident, and you would have thought that by now the disciples would get Jesus's mysterious power. But they didn't. They still struggled when it came to their own lives. In the storm, they doubted his empathy and compassion toward them. When Jesus walked on the water, they assumed he was a ghost. When the multitude drew near and Jesus wanted to feed them, the disciples focused more on what they lacked than what God could do.

Have you ever felt that way? Do you trust God to come through for others more than he will for you? Does the size of your problem overshadow the effectiveness of your faith? We have much in common with the disciples, don't we?

Seeing, Hearing, Remembering

Mark 8:14–21 records a striking discussion in which Jesus addresses the disciples' lack of faith and lack of understanding and provides a solution to our confusion when the answer to our why doesn't come. As another day trip unfolds, Jesus uses yeast as a metaphor to describe how religious language and religious behavior can be dangerous when we lack intimacy with God. The disciples, hearing what Jesus says, assume he is confronting them for forgetting to bring bread for their journey. Jesus asks them a why question: "Why are you discussing the fact that you have no bread? Do you not yet perceive or understand? Are your hearts hardened? Having eyes do you not see, and having ears do you not hear? And do you not remember?" (vv. 17–18).

The disciples were with Jesus throughout his ministry, and yet they still completely misunderstood what Jesus was doing. When we, like the disciples, misunderstand who God is and what he can do, we forfeit hope and peace. But God is with us; he shares every moment with us. However, his perspective is often different from ours. He always sees clearly.

And as he did with the disciples, Jesus lovingly confronts us too for our lack of understanding. He asks why we are focused on what we don't have. Faith focuses on what God can do with what we have. Remember the overabundance of food Jesus provided out of a few loaves of bread and some fish.

In that reminder, Jesus addressed the heart of the issue—a lack of understanding and a hardness of heart. Our inability to see God at work has nothing to do with God not being there. Instead, it's about our attitude and whether the eyes of our heart have been opened.

Jesus asks the disciples three questions in a row about seeing, hearing, and remembering. He allows no time for the disciples to respond because he is revealing a truth through mystery.

Imagine Jesus asking you these questions today. First, "Do you not see what's behind the broken world and your hurting life?" At times, or maybe most of the time, your authentic response may be something like, "No, Lord, I really don't see much right now. I know you're supposed to be close. I know you care. Like the disciples, I am aware of countless times you fulfilled your promise. You healed the bleeding woman, brought peace to the tormented, defied the impossible, and even raised the dead. But I don't see any purpose in what I'm going through, nor do I see how you're going to make something beautiful come from it. No, to be honest, I guess I don't see you right now."

The promises of God are accessible to us all, but the alluring voice of hopelessness in the valley seems too convincing. In the middle of the noise, Jesus asks a second question: "Do you not hear?"

To this we might answer, "No, Lord, with all the distractions, suffering, division, and uncertainty, I really don't hear your voice. I pray and cry out and even believe you're there. I know you're inviting me to surrender, trust, and walk intimately with you. But I'm having a hard time hearing your voice. I was created for so much more than just making it through another day. The world longs to see Christ in me, the hope of glory, put on display. But I can't hear you right now because life is just too loud."

Jesus doesn't give up on you when you don't see the burning bush. He doesn't throw you to the side when you don't hear his voice like Philip, Jeremiah, or Abraham did. In his mercy, he gently poses a third question: "But can you remember?" We can all remember what God has done in the past.

When you are sitting with your why questions, it's important to know that you're not alone. Psalm 44:23–24 records the words of someone who was struggling to remember who God was when life became very hard. The psalmist says, "Awake! Why are you sleeping, O Lord? Rouse yourself! Do not reject us forever! Why do you hide your face? Why do you forget our affliction and oppression?" The anonymous writer vulnerably asks God why three times. Each one of the why questions are accusatory, almost as if charging God with a crime. We do not know what or if God ever answered. It isn't recorded. But we can dig into the rest of Scripture for the answers the psalmist probably knew as well.

First, the writer accuses God of sleeping. This question reveals how dire the person's situation seems. Psalm 121:3–4 makes it clear that God never sleeps. The notion that God remains aloof and indifferent in the middle of experiencing heartbreak and suffering is absurd. We know God doesn't nap while our world falls apart. No, God is loving and near, and he desires to bless us (2 Chron. 15:2). He sees us like he saw Hagar.

Second, the psalmist accuses God of hiding his face. This is the same face that God wants to shine upon us described in Numbers 6. No, God wasn't hiding his face. Perhaps the person writing this has drifted so far away that God's face is no longer visible to him.

Third, the writer accuses God of forgetting. However, Scripture is clear that God could never forget our affliction because he bears and carries our sorrows (Isa. 53:11). God won't forget what he carries in his hands.

Once you realize your why questions don't scare God, you can approach him with a different perspective, like David, who wrote Psalm 34. This chapter provides a glimpse of a heart with eyes wide open to God's faithfulness over time. On the other side of so many heartbreaking experiences, some the result of his own decisions and others the result of injustice toward him, David remembered what God had done. During some painful moments when God seemed far away and all seemed lost and ruined, David looked back and saw how immovable and unshakable God's character is, saying, "The LORD is near to the brokenhearted and saves the crushed in spirit" (v. 18). David's uncertainties did not breed hopelessness or anxiety because he chose to remember.

Found

Remember what it was like when you first met God? Remember that time you needed to know what God was feeling, and you opened your Bible and knew the words came straight from God's heart to yours? Remember that tear-soaked prayer, whispered in a voice made hoarse by the multitudes of previous prayers, that forcefully moved heaven to earth? Remember that time, around the bend in the park, when God surprised you and drew near? Remember the time you sensed his divine presence, otherworldly and pure, and it was clearly from him to you? Remember the encouraging text message that came just at the right time, the kindness of the stranger when your hands were full, and the random hug your child gave you that made all the cares of this world fade away? These were divine interruptions, burning bushes, evidence of things hoped for.

There is one moment in my history with God that I go back to often. It is the center of all my beginnings. When I must start somewhere, I start there. The place he found me. That place he refused to let me remain.

When I was seventeen, my life was utterly out of control. I was not a safe person to be around. Years of childhood trauma and the excuses I used to live recklessly redefined what normal was. I had no idea who God was. My experiences laid a faulty foundation for my life. Still, I knew there was something spiritual out there. Though addicted to numerous substances and rarely sober, pulling off good grades was not difficult for me. I liked to learn, and it came easily.

So in my spare time, I learned as much as I could about multiple religions and spiritualities and even created some of my own. I had been to church a few times as a teenager, but I never knew God. I had no room in my life for beliefs that were void of actions. It sounds jaded, but sometimes I found more conviction and truth around drug addicts. Still, I looked for God incessantly. I asked my friends, strangers, and teammates about their beliefs. I had proof and evidence that something, someone, was out there, but I didn't know his name. I was looking for any glimpse of hope that things in my life could change. Then hope found me.

It was a Sunday afternoon when I was a junior in high school. Along with a few friends, I was experimenting with a new substance to dull my senses and create an imaginary world to live in. I sought a world without regret, shame, and the burden of reality, one where everything was supposedly perfect. It was an illusion, but it seemed safe.

Four of us sat in the car at a park. One of my friends took out a small pocket New Testament and started reading a story. Why he read that story I still do not know. He was not a Christian. In fact, he often made fun of them. In all my learning about religion and spirituality, I had never given Jesus full access to my heart.

Mark 5:1–20 tells the story of a man called Legion—a military term the Romans used to describe a cohort of soldiers.

Gadara, the backdrop of the story, was full of limestone caves that were converted to tombs, and it was rumored to be home to spirits of the underworld. We don't know the man's real name, but Legion lived among the tombs and was known to be haunted by evil spirits. He self-mutilated, was often unclothed, and couldn't be subdued, which explains why the townspeople were terrified of him.

Jesus and some of his disciples arrived by boat on the shores of Gadara. When Legion saw Jesus from a distance, he ran to him. The face of God transformed this man entirely. The change was so complete that others struggled to reconcile the man with the one they knew from the tombs.

After reading the story, my friend wanted to know who we thought Jesus was. He put his opinion out there first and dogmatically declared Jesus was a spiritual guru. One of my other buddies argued with him, making his opinion abundantly clear that Jesus was a reincarnated Native American warrior. I sat there, enjoying the substances flowing through my veins, and listened to them go back and forth. Then my best friend at the time spoke up and shared the gospel with all of us. He was raised in a gospel-believing home. His personal life didn't match what he said he believed, but as he shared, I sobered up and my heart listened intently. Coupled with all the other spiritual beliefs I had learned about over the years, that day my soul became very curious about Jesus.

That night as I lay in bed alone, wide awake and, despite the methamphetamines in my bloodstream, fully sober, I couldn't stop thinking about who Jesus was. I remembered conversations I'd had with my lab partner in physics class who shared the gospel with me. I remembered my conversations about God with my future wife Ali, and the few times I'd gone to church with her. I felt like Legion: exposed, tormented, covered bodily with evidence of a hard life lived. In my heart, I knew if I too ran to Jesus, he wouldn't turn me away. He wouldn't be embarrassed to be seen with me. All the information collided at once, like a million seeds scattered across the surface of my heart that, over time, settled deep down inside and took hold. At just the right time, God sent the rain, and those seeds of faith bloomed.

It is hard to find the words to describe what happened. That's usually the way it works with God. What I do know is hope found me that cold, wintry Sunday night in Iowa. I said Jesus's name out loud and finally met him. Liquid peace dripped from the sky and slowly, meticulously, washed away the spiritual death I'd accumulated in my life. What happened is still a mystery to me—a miracle.

A few days later, after wandering into a small church, I publicly confessed before God who I was and, more importantly, who Jesus is. I surrendered my life to Jesus. That was the beginning of a new story God would write. Jesus loved me, forgave me, and he is more real now, decades later, than he has ever been. When I have a hard time seeing and hearing spiritually, I remember who God is and who he has always been, starting with when I met him at seventeen.

Back in the beginning, in the garden of Eden, Adam and Eve ate from the tree of the knowledge of good and evil. They sought knowledge, understanding, and the ability and capacity to make accurate assessments about everything.

The expansion of understanding was attractive to them, and frankly, even now it doesn't seem like a morally corrupt desire. But they deliberately did something God had told them not to do. They were on a quest to know something God hadn't revealed to them. For this reason, they eventually exalted their desire over God's, and they ate the fruit from the tree of the knowledge of good and evil.

God can handle it when we ask why with the desire to know what we currently do not know. But this desire in Adam and Eve grew. It metastasized and was powerful enough to seduce them away from a perfect relationship with God. Knowing why isn't worth that price.

Uncertainty and ambiguity don't have to be negatives in our lives. Having every situation reconciled or figured out will not bring peace. When knowing why permanently takes up real estate in our hearts, we not only forfeit peace that transcends understanding; we take our own bite of the fruit of the tree we're not meant to eat.

I still face uncertainties, experience the pain of loss, and am sometimes distracted from my spiritual inheritance by hopelessness. I may not have answers to all my whys, but I remember when hope found me in my darkest hour. If God can find me then and there, I no longer need to know the whys of mysteries. They don't matter because I know God.

If you don't already have an indescribable moment with God to look back on, remember how God loved the one called Legion. As he did for that shamed, self-harming man, God will meet you right where you are. He will accept you in your worst place and then walk with you, even carry you, toward your very own future and hope.

He Still Knows

As I finish this chapter, I'm on a sixteen-hour flight headed to the best part of any trip—being back at home with my family. Without their prayers and support, I wouldn't be able to share with you what God, and only God, is doing through the power of hope. This book is full of stories from trips I've taken. People regularly say that traveling like this seems adventurous and exciting. It is not always as fun as it sounds.

My travels often take me to precarious and heartbreaking places where the realities of injustice need to be confronted with the only hope that will endure. It can be complex and difficult, and some of the things I see stick with me. Then there's also missing family meals, not hearing the laughter, being stuck in airports because of another unforeseen delay, and not sleeping well. While travel isn't my idea of grand living, it is part of what God invited us into. I trust it will be another offering to give him when eternity begins one day.

People also talk about the work I and the rest of the team at Convoy of Hope are doing. To many it seems heroic. I just think we are being obedient to what God is asking of us. God puts his love for humanity on display through the simple acts of obedience from ordinary people like you and me. The real hero of the story is God. It is God and God alone who knocks on the door of human hearts. When we open the door, we are invited to partner with him in what only he can do in our lives and the lives of others. Hope only works when it is tethered to God.

On this trip, though, I experienced another divine interruption. I guess you could say I was having a hard time seeing and hearing. But God gave me another moment to remember one day.

We were in the poorest, most vulnerable region of Tanzania. We arrived in one of the villages where Convoy of Hope works. The people gathered around and welcomed us with singing and dancing. One song was written just for us, expressing gratitude for the small part we played in what

God did among them. After hearing stories of how the God of hope transformed their lives, how their children were no longer hungry, and how sustainable sources of food, water, and income were their new reality, the bishop of the region prayed for us.

We stood in a circle and I closed my eyes. As he prayed, I felt something brush my left shoulder. Assuming it was a bird or a swarm of flies, I ignored it. Then something brushed up against my lower left leg. This time, I assumed it was a goat. A shadow then cast over the left side of my face and, sensing something or someone drawing near, I opened my eyes. A hand came down on my left shoulder. I turned to find a man dressed in his ancestral tribal clothing, who then wrapped his arm around me. I reciprocated and we stood that way until the prayer concluded. At the end of the prayer, the man spoke passionately to me through a translator.

Born blind, Himani does not know the difference between green or red. He hasn't seen the miraculous pink-and-blue sunsets over the African plains. He is blind but, in many ways, he sees much better than I do. He shared how a few days prior, God came to him in a dream and said to go to that particular village on that particular day at that specific time, because people of God were there. As he approached the village, he said God told him there was a leader he was supposed to find. He recalled how God spoke in his heart specific directions, when to go right or left, leading him directly to me. Being told by God to stop, he searched for me. What I felt on my shoulder and leg was his hand and staff trying to find me.

God led Himani directly to me. Little did he know that, on that day in the middle of nowhere, I was deeply discouraged. I've seen miracle after miracle take place over the years. I have observed one impossibility after another bow its knee to God. But somehow, someway, even after everything I've seen and heard on my journey with God, I'd forgotten.

Discouragement knocks on everyone's door from time to time. On that day I opened it and found myself distracted by life's troubles. That morning, before we ventured out, I remember saying, "God, I just need to know. I just need to know that you see me." And hope found me again because a blind man dared to listen when God spoke. Willing to look foolish for the sake of obedience, he trusted God step-by-step, not knowing how God would work through his surrender, trust, and intimacy with the Father.

God loves Himani as much as he loves me. I doubt the entire situation was orchestrated by God just for me. Who knows what else God was up to? Perhaps God was working to encourage Himani. Maybe the other villagers needed to see that sometimes we literally walk by faith and not always by sight. With the eyes of his heart opened, Himani saw clearly, and we both felt a sense of awe and wonder at how God brought our paths together. God reminded me that day of what I knew all along. I just needed to remember.

Every now and then, we all need reminders that we are still seen like Hagar and are still capable of traversing the rubble like Nehemiah. If God can do something remarkable through a tentmaker's handkerchief and apron, like he did with Paul in the ancient city of Ephesus, he can work miracles through our lives as well. God gives us clear moments of his presence so that when we don't see or hear, we can still remember.

As we were driving away from the village, I remembered that day in my junior year of high school in Iowa and how the God of hope found me when I was lost. Just then, my heart heard God's whisper, just like I'm sure Himani heard: "I still know where to find you."

When you place your hope in God, he will always break through and find you too.

ACKNOWLEDGMENTS

The grace and mercy of God are indescribable. This is for him and to him.

The support of my wife, Ali, and our daughters, Leighton and Dallon, has been unconditional and undeserved. Thank you for all of your prayers, sacrifice, and encouragement. I love you.

The team at Convoy of Hope works relentlessly to put the kindness of God on display around the world. It is an honor to serve with all of you.

Thank you to Baker Books and Christopher Ferebee for believing in this project and for your collaboration.

NOTES

Chapter 1 A Desperate Need for Hope

1. Morgan Phillips, "Arkansas Woman Texted Father's Number Every Day After He Died, She Got a Response Four Years Later," Fox News, updated October 26, 2019, https://www.foxnews.com/us/arkansas-woman-texting-father-every-day-response.

2. Kirsten Weir, "Mission Impossible," *American Psychological Association* 44, no. 9 (October 2013), https://www.apa.org/monitor/2013/10/mission-impossible.

3. L. A. Curry et al., "Role of Hope in Academic and Sport Achievement," *Journal of Personality and Social Psychology* 73, no. 6 (December 1997): 1257–67, https://pubmed.ncbi.nlm.nih.gov/9418279/.

4. Brené Brown, *Atlas of the Heart: Mapping Meaningful Connection and the Language of Human Experience* (Random House, 2021), 97.

5. Brown, *Atlas of the Heart*, 101.

6. Peter L. Berger, *A Rumor of Angels: Modern Society and the Rediscovery of the Supernatural* (Anchor Books, 1970), 4.

7. Claudia Bloeser and Titus Stahl, s.v. "Hope," *Stanford Encyclopedia of Philosophy*, updated March 21, 2022, https://plato.stanford.edu/entries/hope/.

8. Arthur C. Brooks, "The Difference Between Hope and Optimism," *The Atlantic*, September 23, 2021, https://www.theatlantic.com/family/archive/2021/09/hope-optimism-happiness/620164/.

9. *The Poems of Emily Dickinson*, ed. R. W. Franklin (Harvard University Press, 1999), https://www.poetryfoundation.org/poems/42889/hope-is-the-thing-with-feathers-314.

10. Bloeser and Stahl, s.v. "Hope."

11. Bloeser and Stahl, s.v. "Hope."

12. Henry Cloud, "The difference between hopping [sic] and wishing is that hope comes from real, objective reasons," Facebook, January 14, 2019, https://www.facebook.com/DrHenryCloud/posts/the-difference -between-hopping-and-wishing-is-that-hope-comes-from-real-objectiv /10157064384234571/.

13. Caroline Leaf, *Switch On Your Brain: The Key to Peak Happiness, Thinking, and Health* (Baker Books, 2013), 32.

14. Leaf, *Switch On Your Brain*, 33.

15. Leaf, *Switch On Your Brain*, 26.

16. *Strong's Exhaustive Concordance*, "tiqvah," https://biblehub.com /strongs/hebrew/8615.htm.

17. *Strong's Exhaustive Concordance*, "tiqvah."

18. *Brown-Driver-Briggs Hebrew Lexicon*, "ra'ah," https://www .bibletools.org/index.cfm/fuseaction/lexicon.show/ID/h7200/page/4.

19. *Brown-Driver-Briggs Hebrew Lexicon*, "ra'ah"; *Bible and Archaeology, University of Iowa*, "ra'ah," https://bam.sites.uiowa.edu/RTL/raah.

Chapter 2 Spiritual Poverty

1. As quoted in David Wemyss, "A Severed Wasp: Orwell–Woolf–Kierkegaard," New English Press, November 2022, https://www.new englishreview.org/articles/a-severed-wasp-orwell-woolf-kierkegaard/.

2. Henri Nouwen, *Bread for the Journey: A Daybook of Wisdom and Faith* (HarperOne, 2006), August 4 entry.

3. For more information, see Clyde E. Fant and Mitchell G. Reddish, *A Guide to Biblical Sites in Greece and Turkey* (Oxford Academic, 2003).

4. Sam Storms, "The Letter to the Church at Laodicea (3:14-22)," Sam Storms, November 1, 2006, https://www.samstorms.org/all-articles/post /the-letter-to-the-church-at-laodicea--3:14-22-.

5. *Englishman's Concordance*, "meleim," https://biblehub.com/greek /4434.htm.

6. Doug Anderson, "Caring for God's Creation: Living Laudato Si'," The Catholic Sun, July 20, 2023, https://thecatholicsun.com/caring-for -gods-creation-living-laudato-si-8/.

Chapter 3 What Is God Like?

1. *Brown-Driver-Briggs Hebrew Lexicon*, "Shaddai," https://www .blueletterbible.org/lexicon/h7706/nlt/wlc/0-1/.

2. Hope Bolinger, "What Does Adonai Mean?," Christianity.com, October 12, 2023, https://www.christianity.com/wiki/god/what-does -adonai-mean.html.

3. *Encyclopaedia Britannica*, "Yahweh," https://www.britannica.com /topic/Yahweh.

4. *Strong's Lexicon*, "bless you," https://biblehub.com/strongs/num bers/6-24.htm.

5. *Strong's Exhaustive Concordance*, "shamar," https://biblehub.com /hebrew/8104.htm.

6. *Strong's Lexicon*, "panim," https://www.blueletterbible.org/lexicon /h6440/kjv/wlc/0-1/.

7. *Strong's Exhaustive Concordance*, "chanan," https://biblehub.com /hebrew/2603.htm.

8. *Strong's Lexicon*, "shalom," https://biblehub.com/strongs/numbers /6-26.htm.

Chapter 4 Change Me First

1. *Oxford Reference Library*, "Adonai," https://www.oxfordreference .com/display/10.1093/oi/authority.20110803100221969.

2. *Brown-Driver-Briggs Hebrew Lexicon*, "male," https://biblehub .com/hebrew/4390.htm.

3. Ernest Hemingway, *A Farewell to Arms* (Scriber, 1995), 249.

4. Michelle Liebst, "The Sultans of Zanzibar and the Abolition of Slavery in East Africa," *Cambridge University Press* 42, no. 1 (2024): 49–72, https://doi.org/10.1017/S0738248023000561; "Zanzibar's Story: Remembering the Past, Securing the Future," World Monuments Fund Britain, accessed January 7, 2024, https://www.wmf.org/sites/default /files/article/pdfs/Zanzibar%20Exhibition_0.pdf.

5. R. G. Thorne, "Wilberforce, William (1759-1833)," in The History of Parliament: The House of Commons 1790-1820, ed. R. Thorne (1986), https://www.historyofparliamentonline.org/volume/1790-1820/member /wilberforce-william-1759-1833.

6. Thorne, "Wilberforce, William."

7. "Zanzibar's Story: Remembering the Past, Securing the Future."

Chapter 5 The Eyes of Your Heart

1. T. S. Eliot, "Little Gidding," in *The Complete Poems and Plays 1909–1950* (Harcourt, 1950), 145.

2. Cassie Williams, "Quadriga CEO's Widow Speaks Out over His Death and the Missing Crypto Millions," CBC, January 18, 2022, https:// www.cbc.ca/news/canada/nova-scotia/quadriga-widow-jennifer-robers ton-gerald-cotten-1.6318955.

3. Nicole Pelletiere, "Arizona Grandma, Man She Mistakenly Texted, to Share Thanksgiving for 7th Straight Year Since 2016," Fox News,

November 24, 2022, https://www.foxnews.com/lifestyle/arizona-grandma
-man-she-mistakenly-texted-share-thanksgiving-7th-straight-year-since
-2016.

4. Celina Tebor, "Buffalo Woman Saves Man with Severe Frostbite
After Getting Him Out of the Storm and Pleading for Help in a Facebook
Livestream," CNN, December 28, 2022, https://www.cnn.com/2022/12
/27/us/buffalo-woman-saves-man-frostbite-facebook/index.html.

5. Scott Murray and John Ashdown, "The Knowledge Christmas
Special: Did World War One Matches Really Happen?," *The Guardian*,
December 18, 2012, https://www.theguardian.com/football/2012/dec/19
/the-knowledge-christmas-special.

6. A. J. Baime and Volker Janssen, "WWI's Christmas Truce: When
Fighting Paused for the Holiday," *History*, February 26, 2024, https://
www.history.com/.amp/news/christmas-truce-1914-world-war-i-soldier
-accounts.

7. Walter Brueggemann, *A Gospel of Hope*, compiled by Richard
Floyd (Westminster John Knox Press, 2018), 104–5.

Chapter 6 The Miracle of Endurance

1. Gene Weingarten, "Setting the Record Straight on the Joshua Bell
Experiment," *Washington Post*, October 14, 2014, https://www.washing
tonpost.com/news/style/wp/2014/10/14/gene-weingarten-setting-the-rec
ord-straight-on-the-joshua-bell-experiment/.

2. Anne Azzi Davenport, "Grammy-Winning Violinist Joshua Bell
Delights Masses at DC Subway Concert," PBS News, September 30, 2014,
https://www.pbs.org/newshour/arts/grammy-winning-violinist-joshua
-bell-takes-another-turn-at-a-subway-concert.

3. Brett Zongker, "Violinist Joshua Bell Plays It Again at D.C. Station,"
Detroit Free Press, September 30, 2014, https://www.freep.com/story/enter
tainment/music/2014/09/30/joshua-bell-violinist-train-station/16481377/.

4. *NAS Exhaustive Concordance*, "telos," https://biblehub.com/greek
/5055.htm.

5. Janine Puhak, "College Professor Carries Student's Baby in Class
for 3 Hours, Goes Viral," Fox News, September 26, 2019, https://www
.foxnews.com/lifestyle/college-professor-class-baby.

Chapter 7 Listen Carefully to the Interruption

1. *Merriam-Webster Dictionary*, s.v. "surrender," accessed September
23, 2024, https://www.merriam-webster.com/dictionary/surrender.

2. *Cambridge Dictionary*, s.v. "trust," accessed September 23, 2024,
https://dictionary.cambridge.org/us/dictionary/english/trust.

3. *Merriam-Webster Dictionary*, s.v. "believe," accessed September 23, 2024, https://www.merriam-webster.com/dictionary/believe.

Chapter 8 Remember

1. *Thayer's Greek Lexicon (Strong's G3466)*, "mysterion," https://www.blueletterbible.org/lexicon/g3466/kjv/tr/0-1/.

2. *Thayer's Greek Lexicon (Strong's G3466)*, "musterion," https://www.bibletools.org/index.cfm/fuseaction/Lexicon.show/ID/G3466/musterion.htm.

3. William Shakespeare, *Macbeth*, act 4, scene 3.

HEATH ADAMSON is the author of *Grace in the Valley* and *The Sacred Chase*. As senior vice president of global program at Convoy of Hope, he works with communities to address root causes of poverty and hunger. His PhD is from the University of London. He speaks at universities, conferences, symposiums, and churches. While he often catches a fresh glimpse of what only God can do among the world's most vulnerable, his favorite place to be is with his wife, Ali, and their two daughters, Leighton and Dallon. Heath invites you to embrace the greatest pursuit in life: to cultivate a flourishing, deeply personal, and contagious relationship with Jesus.

CONNECT WITH HEATH:

HeathAdamson.com